CRACKS
CREVICES
&
DIRT

Exposing the Lies That Prevent Us from Trusting God

ALICIA H. WATSON

Cracks, Crevices, and Dirt:
Exposing The Lies that Prevent
Us from Trusting God

ISBN: 0692743359

ISBN-13: 978-0692743355

Editing by SermonAssist

DEDICATION

I dedicate this book in loving memory of my parents, Esther Bell-Watson and John E. Watson. There is not a day that goes by that I do not think about you both. Thank you for your prayers, your love, and your support. I know you're in heaven singing and ministering with all of God's angels.

TABLE OF CONTENTS

ACKNOWLEDGMENTS

To my Lord and Savior, Jesus Christ. Thank you for believing in me. Thank you for establishing these great gifts you have given me in this world. Jesus, I thank you for being my confidant, my best friend, my mother, my father, and most of all, the greatest reflection of God's love for me. Thank you for entrusting me with this gift. Lord, I thank you for divinely writing this book through me. I thank you that the words you have written will bring revelation knowledge to all those who read it.

To my pastors, Dr. Creflo Dollar and Pastor Taffi Dollar, thank you for your consistent teaching of the Word. Thank you for teaching on the grace and favor of God when I needed it most. Most importantly, thank you for being obedient to birthing the concept of a "World Changer." Thank you for teaching us that with Jesus, we can change the world.

To my spiritual family, Bishop Kent Branch and Pastor Diana Branch, I acknowledge the great role you have played in my life. Our relationship was divine and through your love and support, I learned to overcome every obstacle that was placed before me. Thank you for the years of teaching, servanthood, and prayer that you instilled in me.

To Minister Michael L. Owens, you have been a tremendous leader to me. You pulled gifts and talents out of me that I never knew I possessed. Thank you for always pushing me in the things of God. Thank you for all the moments where you loved me like a daughter. To Mrs. Shemika Owens, thank you for your warm embrace. Thank you for the many tight hugs that were filled with so much love that every time I think of you, I think of God's love for me.

To Pastors Lathan and Kelli Wood, it was that day I joined the VOP Gospel choir that forever changed my life. I met Jesus in those rehearsals, and you both poured so much life into me. I would not be here without both of you. Pastor Lathan, thank you for taking the twelve of us and pulling us close to you. You saved our lives.

To my podcast mentor, Terri Savelle Foy, thank you for teaching me that I could achieve my goals. Thank you for your podcasts on discipline and strategy. Your words helped me turn this book into a reality. Thank you for being a beacon of light for all of us who did not initially believe in the gifts that God placed inside of us.

To Youth Pastors, Anthony and Constance Adams, thank you for your unending support and love! You both are the most encouraging ministers that I know. I appreciate you for every prayer, every phone call to check on me and most of all the agape love you both show towards me.

To my sisters, Fly Musiq, Camille, Taheerah, Doll, and Courtney, I could not have written this book without your love and support. Thank you for listening to all my ideas and helping me navigate into my purpose for writing. Thank you for being the first ones to share my blogs or affirm my gifts. Most importantly, thank you for your friendship and sisterhood.

To my family, the Bells, Campbell's and Hunt's thank you for sticking with me throughout all of my processes. Thank you for watching me evolve into the woman I am today, and being accepting of what God has placed in me. Thank you for adopting me into your homes and families, when my parents died. Thank you for teaching me the Word and the power of forgiveness. Uncle Jonny and Aunt Carolyn, thank you for every word of encouragement and correction. Thank you for teaching me the Word and the power of forgiveness. I would not be who I am without you. Thank you for accepting me into your home and your life.

To Aunt Naomi, thank you for being a voice of reason. Thank you for always knowing what to say to encourage me. I acknowledge the gifts that God has placed in you, and I appreciate the wisdom you've spoken to me throughout life. Thank you for being a gentle reminder of my mother. I appreciate you telling me stories of who she was because it helped me to know who I am. To Aunt Pam and Aunt Monica, thank you for your words of wisdom and encouragement. Thank you for your support and for accepting me completely. I appreciate you both so much!

To all of my online family, extended family, and friends, I love you all. Thank you for sharing your comments and for building my confidence as a writer. Every hug or word of encouragement has led me to this moment. Special thanks to Rhenardo Worrell, for helping me birth the title of this book, and encouraging me to get it finished.

INTRODUCTION

Have you ever been lied to? Do you remember how it felt when you found out the truth? Were you upset, frustrated, or numb to the situation? Or perhaps, you have told a lie to someone. Did your lies ever just end with one lie or did you have to keep lying to guard the first lie you told? Were you angry with yourself for lying or angry at the person who lied to you?

I am asking you all of these questions because when I was younger, I was a very creative liar. I was manipulative, calculated, and a wonderful actress for all those who viewed my emotional shows. I could control any situation to get what I wanted because I was talented in my false imagination. I can remember my aunt telling me that I told more stories (lies) than a storybook. She would make me read the scriptures on how God detested lying, and I would stutter to read through them feeling inadequate as a human.

I felt like I was God's biggest mistake on this earth. There I was, an orphan at the age of fifteen and feeling useless. My lies would always get me into trouble. Afterward, I would feel horrible and ask God to kill me so that I would not hurt or offend anyone else. I can remember lying on my closet floor at the age of sixteen, praying that God would allow me to take my last breath. I did not want this life that I was given, and I begged Him to take me to heaven too, just like He had taken my mother and father.

For years, I believed that I was God's only mistake. Somehow, He had forgotten about me and all the trouble I would cause those around me. Thoughts of suicide and depression plagued my mind as I struggled after the death of my parents. Not only had my parents died in the worst way possible, but their deaths made me feel like the people I loved died because of me. In addition to this thought concept, unfortunately, I treated my mother poorly when she was dying because I was numb from all the pain I felt inside. For some reason, I believed that I could prepare myself for her death by pretending that she was already dead. Looking back, I realize how dumb that concept was. By the time she finally went on to be with Jesus, I was devastated and no one understood why.

Through it all, I never thought about the fact that I have an adversary who roams the earth seeking whom he can devour and destroy. So, I believed I was evil, not realizing that my bad attitude and cold heart were simply from all the hell I had experienced in my life that no one knew. I did not understand that God had a plan for my life and everything I had experienced would work out for my good.

On the outside, my parents and I were the happiest family, but on the inside, we were all boiling with rage and anger. No one ever thought to ask me what was wrong with me or why I had shut down to all those who were around me. No one ever thought about how my actions as a teenager were from all the hurt and loss I had experienced. Instead, they judged my behavior, not understanding that it was a symptom of much deeper issues. No one knew how badly I starved for real hugs and kisses. No one knew how much I craved for someone to love me and accept me because I felt so alone. No one understood how the death of my parents and the lies that surrounded our lives had affected me internally as a person. Looking back, I realize that the Devil wanted me dead, and he was pulling out every tactic in his book to destroy me before I even had a chance.

My parents were all I had. As I said earlier—on the outside we were the perfect family, however on the inside, it was a different story. No one knew that my parents would argue frequently. My first recollection of their loud arguments was when I was five-years-old. This is when I noticed a significant change in my life. I remember my mother and father screaming at the top of their lungs facing each other with what seemed like hatred in their eyes. It was not long before I concluded that their fighting was because of me. This was the first lie from the Devil that I believed. My father used to always tell me that they only stayed together because of me, not knowing that his comment would breed a web of lies in my mind.

When the fights got really bad, my mother would take me to a hotel room with her for the night. I guess it was her way of teaching my father a lesson and making him realize that if she left, she was taking me with her. Not even six years old, yet, I was already a pawn in this marital war where they both sought the winning hand. I remember being angry about how much they argued but also thinking that it was normal. I figured all couples argued like that and perhaps, that is how you show love to someone. I thought it was normal to fight behind closed doors and pretend to be happy in front of everyone else.

As I grew older, I grew weary and frustrated with always being put in the center of their arguments. The inability to express this to them only deepened my belief that my existence had caused such intense hatred between them. Since I could not control my home life, I sought to control my outside life by creating my own reality. This is when I started lying and realizing that I could manipulate people to give me the affection I craved because what I received at home did not seem genuine or real.

My parents met in Washington, D.C. where they both worked in a copyright office. Their love and passion for music and God brought them together. Looking at the pictures, they looked so happy and in love with each other. I believe they dated for a while and decided to marry quickly. I am told that my mother's family was a little skeptical of my father and so they advised my mother to wait and get to know him better. However, like anyone in love, you do not always listen to the wisdom of others.

My father was a very talented and well-known man in gospel music. While musically serving in the Catholic church, he was invited to Rome, Italy to orchestrate a mass for Pope John Paul II. This was the highlight of his career. So, at the age of one, I accompanied my parents as we traveled across the world for ministry. After the presentation of the mass, Pope John Paul II saw me and blessed me. Looking back, it was such a blessing for a little African American baby to be blessed by the pope himself. I'd like to think that this blessing was just God's way of saying that He had His hands on me.

A few years later, I would wake up one morning to find my father unconscious. Not knowing that my father had contracted the HIV virus from an extramarital relationship with a priest in our church. Also, not knowing that he had infected my mother and that they would both die quickly from full blown AIDS in less than five years.

All those years, I thought they were arguing about me when they were really arguing about my father's infidelity. All those years, the Devil convinced me to believe that I was the source of their unhappiness and chaotic relationship. All those years, I blamed myself for something that had absolutely nothing to do with me. When I review the situation, I realize how the Devil will have you blame yourself for something that you had no control over just to keep you from seeing who God truly created you to be.

I grew up believing that I was a liar and that there was no hope for someone like me. After all, the bad things that were happening in my life were directly related to the people I loved. Burying my mother on my 15th birthday, was the most traumatic experience I have ever had in my life. Realizing that my father cheated on my mother with a man, was heartbreaking and shocking. Seeing my parents fight for their lives, struggling to conquer an incurable disease left so much suffering and sorrow in my heart that there are no words to adequately describe what I was feeling on the inside. Lies were created and engrained in my soul that caused a negative outlook on me and others.

I tell you all of that to help you understand why I have decided to write this book. This book is not solely about my life, but it is about exposing the dark and dirty secrets in our lives so that we can be free to live the life God has promised us. Keeping the secret of my family was more internally damaging than it was externally. Until one day, I decided that God was my only source, and I had to trust in Him. Through a process of healing, God eliminated the cracks in my faith, the crevices of darkness that kept me paralyzed, and the shame of dirt I carried from the past.

We have an adversary, and his name is Satan. The Bible says he is roaming the earth, seeking whom he can devour. He is actively looking, searching, and hunting for anyone who will accept his lies and his reasoning. He is actively pursuing you—his goal is simply to destroy the assignment God has on your life.

I share my story with you because I want you to see the power of God's grace. Now, in my thirties, I am free from the past, and I walk in complete forgiveness concerning every hurt, loss, and frustration I incurred early in life. As a believer, we all want to trust God completely, but we are unable to do so until we are willing to expose every lie that the Devil and life experiences have influenced us to believe. Whenever unbelief is present in our lives, there is a lie present that we have believed. We can never move past what we are unwilling to expose.

Each chapter of this book shares personal stories of victory and tragedy in my own life. After experiencing loss at an early age, I knew I wanted to help people.

Through years of study and life lessons, God has taught me about faith, and what it truly means to believe.

Faith is more than just a scripture. It is a mindset. It is a belief that you guard higher than anything. Faith says that anything is possible. Anything short of this belief has been impacted by unbelief, doubt, worry, or fear. Your faith is a weapon. It is a tool that God has freely given every man. By faith, the woman with the issue of blood was healed. By faith, Job was restored. By faith, I wrote this book. Anything is truly possible—if you BELIEVE!

My Prayer For You

Holy Spirit, guide the readers through this book with revelation knowledge. Speak through my words and minister to their situations. God illuminate their minds with strategies and wisdom to become everything you have created them for in this life. Lord, free them from fear, doubt, guilt, worry, regret, shame, and anything in their pasts that prevent them from walking in their true authority as Christian believers. Jesus, I believe that anything is possible with you. I believe that you have led them to this book for a reason. I add my faith with theirs for whatever they are believing God for spiritually, emotionally, physically, mentally, and supernaturally. Lord, I thank you that everything they need is available in your finished works. Jesus, I thank you for what you are about to do in them and through them. I bind every demonic and satanic force that would hinder them from their assignment in this life, and I release your authority and power as sole ruler over their lives. Father, expose every lie in their belief system that is contrary to your Word and lead them in truth into the best years of their lives. In Jesus name, I pray, Amen.

-Alicia H. Watson-

CHAPTER 1

Lies He Tells

"A believed lie is enough to destroy your faith."

A lie is something that is untrue. In fact, it is the opposite of the truth. All lies start with a whisper or suggestion in the mind. The Devil is so fascinated with your mind and your thinking that he seeks to influence it by any means possible. He specializes in crafty suggestions in your mind just to see if you will believe them. The moment you believe them or actually say them out of your mouth is the moment he begins fashioning his lies into your foundation.

The goal is simply to get you to question or reconsider what God and His Word have said. When God says "He gave His only Son because He loves you," the Devil comes right behind that thought and says, "Well, if God loved you, would He allow all these bad things to happen to you?" Or when God says that "You are fearfully and wonderfully made," and you look in the mirror and all of a sudden you hear, "If God designed you, He must have messed up, He made so many other people more attractive than you!"

In my case, instead of believing that God loved me, I began to believe that I was God's only mistake. After losing my parents, I could not understand why I had been born just to see them die. In my mind, with the help of the Devil and his lies, I believed that I was a "bad seed." I truly believed that I was the cause of their demise.

Examining the Source of a Lie

Now, let's examine something. What would make a fifteen-year-old believe that the death of her parents is her fault? Where does a lie like that come from? Where does a child learn to blame him or herself for something they could not control? The answer is the Devil. The Devil is the father of all lies. There is no truth in him. In John 8:44, the Bible states that when the Devil speaks, there is no truth in him because he is a liar and the father of all lies and half-truths. Just like God has a plan for your life, the Devil has a plan of destruction for your life as well. And, he is always actively seeking for a way to destroy.

Lies are meant to enslave you into a paralyzing process that limits or destroys your progression in life. The Devil's job is to infiltrate your thinking, enslave you into hurt, fear, worry, unbelief, perversion, pride, habitual cycles, and generational iniquities. Within every lie is a seed of destruction that seeks to imprison you into the kingdom of darkness, keeping you completely blinded from the truth.

Here is a common list of lies we believe:

Lie	Truth	Scripture
You'll never make it through this.	With God all things are possible.	Matthew 19:26 Philippians 4:13
You are forgotten.	God never forgets His children and the work He has begun in us.	Jeremiah 1:5 John 3:16 Hebrews 6:10
You are a mistake.	You were created with a purpose in the image of God.	Philippians 1:6
You will always be broken-hearted.	God binds up all the wounds of the broken heart.	Psalm 147:3 Isaiah 41:10
You are alone.	You are never alone.	Isaiah 41:10 Psalm 27:10 I Samuel 12:22
No one loves you.	God loves you.	Romans 8:38-39 I John 4:10-12 John 3:16

Lie	Truth	Scripture
This situation is impossible.	Nothing is too hard for God.	Philippians 4:13 Genesis 28:15
God does not care about you or your desires.	God is fully aware of your desires and wants to perfect everything that concerns you.	Psalm 138:8 Psalm 37:4 John 15:7
God doesn't hear your prayers.	God hears every prayer.	I John 5:14-15 I John 3:22
You will always fail.	God is confident of the work He has begun in you.	Philippians 1:6 Psalm 34:19
God does not answer prayer.	When you pray, believe that you have already received it.	Mark 11:24 Matthew 21:22 Philippians 4:6 Jeremiah 33:3
You will never be healed.	Jesus took care of healing on the cross. By His stripes we are healed.	Jeremiah 17:4 3 John 2 Mark 16:17-18 Isaiah 53:5
I'm alone.	You are never alone. God is with you. Hope in Him.	Galatians 6:9 Psalm 62:5 Isaiah 40:31

The Influence of Lies in Your Imagination

God loved us so much that He made us in His image. He gave us the ability to create with our imagination, just as He created the earth with His. If we can see it in our minds, we can produce it in reality. Our mental foresight or imagination is the first step to trusting and to believing that what we visualize in our minds can actually be produced in our lives. Before your house was your home, it was just a blueprint that someone imagined. Before your job was a source of financial income, it was just an idea that someone had to make money. Everything in this world began with someone's imagination.

Unlike us, the enemy does not have the power of imagination, so he seeks to infiltrate ours so that he can create his vision for the world. When people choose to operate in darkness or not in the will of God, they are actively yielding and releasing the power of their imagination and the power to create to the Devil. The Devil is not a creator, but he is a perverter or polluter. He aims to taint or influence every thought so that he can see the manifestation of his kingdom, instead of God's kingdom.

One way to identify if a lie is present in your belief system is if you feel fear, unbelief, worry, doubt, anxiety, frustration, anger, resentment, bitterness, unforgiveness, or depression. If the Devil can simply get you to meditate on a lie, he can successfully keep you paralyzed, aggravated, and discontented with your life and with God.

The Crack of a Lie

When we believe a lie, we invite the enemy into our minds and give him creative control to expand his influence into our thoughts. Believing that I was a "bad seed" as a child later influenced my perspective about my identity in Christ, which significantly influenced my ability to trust in God. I often felt that I had to prove myself to others and that I had to work hard to show people that I was a good person. Because I did not believe that I was great enough in life, it caused me to question if I was deserving of the blessings that were in my life. Losing so much at an early age, cracked my foundation of freely being able to trust in God.

All the Devil needs is your belief in one lie he has presented. One untruth is enough to crack a foundation of faith and one half-truth is enough to get us to question whether or not something is true. All it takes is one lie or "what if" question that will lead our minds into a pondering ocean of questions. Once the enemy has opened a door into your thinking, he can influence you to make decisions based upon something that is untrue. Doing this can send you down a dark road in life that hinders you from your true purpose and calling.

When God gave us the power to imagine, it was for His glory. He made man in His image to be like Him. The Devil wanted to be a God, and never achieved that goal. So, he uses us to fulfill his selfish desires. He figures that since he will never be God and never have the power to create, he can influence the ones whom God blessed to create.

The Truth About Your Role in Faith

The only thing God needs us to do in faith is to receive Jesus Christ as our Lord and Savior, receive the Holy Spirit, meditate and be obedient to His Word. God does not need you to do anything else. He only requires that when you do believe, you only believe in His Word and promises, unmoved by what you see, hear, and feel. Faith requires us to believe the Word of God only.

Today, you may be facing a difficult situation. Perhaps, you are looking for answers because it seems you are losing in life. Your present surroundings may say that "things are getting worse," but faith says "God, you said that you will perfect everything that concerns me." Which thought will you rest in? Will you rest in what you see? Or will you rest in what God promised?

I want you to know that your thoughts impact your decisions. Your decisions influence your actions and every action has a positive or negative consequence. The Devil knows that if he wants to influence your life, he just needs to influence your mind. If he has access to your mind, he has access to your thoughts. If he can access your thoughts, he can impact your decisions. If he has access to your decisions, he can destroy you. This process establishes a crack in your faith, which we will discuss in detail in the next chapter.

Chapter Summary

The enemy is a liar. There is no truth in him. His goal is to kill, steal, and destroy you by any means necessary. The enemy uses lies or questionings of God's Word to get us to doubt what God has promised to us. Through this process, we birth resentment, anger, bitterness, hurt, pride, rejection, and so much more. God wants us to know that He gave us the power of imagination to believe in His Word only. Our imagination or the field of the mind can be used to produce good thoughts or negative thoughts. We choose what we will meditate on. We choose what seeds of thought will grow in our minds. We cannot allow our faith to be cracked by unbelief. In summary, we must choose to trust God only.

Study Scriptures

"The thief comes only in order to steal and kill and destroy. I came that they may have and enjoy life, and have it in abundance [to the full, till it overflows]"

John 10:10 (AMP)

"Why do you misunderstand what I am saying? It is because [your spiritual ears are deaf and] you are unable to hear [the truth of] My word. 44 You are of your father the devil, and it is your will to practice the desires [which are characteristic] of your father. He was a murderer from the beginning, and does not stand in the truth because there is no truth in him. When he lies, he speaks what it natural to him, for he is a liar and the father of lies and half-truths. 45 But because I speak the truth, you do not believe Me [and continue in your unbelief]"

John 8:43-45 (AMP)

CHAPTER 2

The Crack of Unbelief

"A crack left untouched eventually shatters."

Have you ever had a crack in your car window? Perhaps, you were driving down the road and a small rock hit your windshield. At first, you may not even have even noticed the small nick in the glass but on the next day, you discover a small chip. One week later, that same chip has expanded all the way across the windshield. Sound familiar?

A crack is a breach in a surface. It is a small hole or line that forms after impact with an object. Cracks begin small and eventually become a threat to the foundation. A driver cannot continue to drive with a crack in the window because eventually, it will expand and become deeper by cutting through the entire depth of the glass. As the crack spreads across the windshield and breaks through the glass, the driver's life becomes endangered. Driving a car with a cracked windshield is hazardous because at any moment the glass can shatter causing an accident or serious injury to everyone inside the car.

Just like a crack in a windshield, unbelief is a crack in your faith and trust in God. It affects how you see yourself, the world, and most importantly, God. When your spiritual perception of faith and trust is breached, it leaves room for the manifestation of unbelief and distrust in God.

The root of unbelief is a lie. When you analyze it, you find that somewhere in your thinking, you have believed a lie over God's Word. Sometimes, it comes in the form of a question. You begin asking if what God has said is really true for you and your situation. Whatever the cause may be, a small or large crack in your faith is enough to prevent you from trusting in God.

When we have unexplainable hurts, losses, betrayals, and overall painful situations in our lives, we give the Devil open access to our beliefs and what we believe is true. Like a poison, unbelief spreads and develops into a massive crack that hinders spiritual growth and supernatural manifestation. If we allow the crack in our faith to expand, it will eventually shatter our expectations and faith in God's Word and His promises for our lives. Ultimately, causing us to question the Word of God and who God is.

Questioning God

When my parents died, I had a lot of questions for God. I did not understand how the losses that I experienced in life would somehow work for my good. I was hurt and frustrated with the pain of the loss, so, I blamed God, not understanding that I was blaming my only source. After watching my parents spiritually, emotionally, and physically wither into death, I felt numb and lifeless. Watching them fight for life was exhausting and mentally draining. I wondered how a God who loved me could allow me to endure so much. Didn't God know that the weight of it all was too much for me to bear? How could a God that promised me abundant life, take the life of my mother away from me? If God was a God of love, where was His love when I needed it most? And, did God even love me?

These questions plagued my young mind. All of the good things I thought about God and His will were now questionable because I lacked complete understanding. Looking back, I realize that my relationship with God was submissive, not relational.

Having a lack of knowledge of God and how He worked caused me to doubt God's ability to provide everything I needed in life. Over the years, as I grew in faith and in the Word, I learned that the death of my parents did not mean that God loved me any less than what His Word said. Through revelation knowledge, I grew to comprehend that my parents made choices that affected our family unit.

In fact, when we experience loss or extreme hurt in life, it does not mean that it was God's divine will. Sometimes, people die before their time due to disobedience or the consequences of their choices. It is important to note that sin is the gateway to spiritual, mental, emotional, or physical death. It does not mean that all illnesses or issues are rooted in sin, there are consequences to every decision and as people, we have to use the wisdom and guidance of the Holy Spirit to lead our lives away from destruction. When my father made a decision to have an affair, he opened the door to destruction in his life. His choice had an unforeseen consequence and what was a moment of passion and lust for him, turned into a gateway of chaos and devastation for our family. That one choice he made affected and changed our lives forever. Isn't it amazing how one bad choice can change the trajectory of our lives?

The Truth About God's Love

God loves us so much, and He gives us the power of choice. He does not force us into a relationship with Him, but He gives us the opportunity to choose if we want to invite Him to be a part of our lives. When we choose to sin and invite sin into our lives, we are handing the Devil an open invitation to destroy us. When we step into sin, we are allowing ourselves to indulge in an activity that was never designed for us. The good thing about God is that He extends His grace or unmerited favor towards us, giving us the opportunity to see the truth and make fruitful decisions in our lives.

When we have unbelief in our lives, it identifies the cracks in our belief system. If we pick and choose what we believe about the Word of God, we lessen the impact of God's power and authority in our lives. God requires our faith and belief in Him, to trust Him and His divine process concerning our destiny.

Finding a Crack in My Belief

My mother was an anointed songstress. With one note, she could bring the congregation to tears. At her funeral, I decided that I would embrace the musical legacy that she and my father left me, and I sang her favorite song in front of the mourning crowd. It was the first time I sang in front of people since my father had passed away. That day, I made a decision that I would be like her and continue her legacy of praise and worship. A few years later, I got the opportunity to lead a song at church. I was so excited that I went home and told everyone.

On that Sunday, when I opened my mouth to sing, I felt the Holy Spirit. It was the first time I felt the warm and tingly sensation of God, and I was so excited. As I led the praise song, looking at the congregation clapping and worshipping Jesus, my eyes stumbled upon some members of my family who sat there with a look of disgust on their faces. Immediately, fear gripped me, and I knew that I had done something wrong. Later that day, I was told that my family was embarrassed. They believed that I had messed up the song by doing too many ad-libs. I was heartbroken.

They also didn't understand how someone who lied as much as me, could get on a pulpit and sing praises to God. I was confused at how the people in the congregation were so proud of me, but my own family was disgusted with me. From that day forward, I started to believe that my gift was not in music. It is sad to believe that one moment created a deep crack in my faith concerning the gift God had placed in me to sing in praise and worship.

Years later, as an adult, I was chosen to lead praise and worship in my church. Our music director believed that he saw a gift in me for leading the people of God into worship. Looking back, I was grown now, mature, saved, and living for God totally.

I had forgotten about the situation that happened as a teenager until the microphone was in my hand. I would like to tell you that I did a good job leading that song, but I completely butchered it. My notes were wrong, my voice was shaky, and overall it did not bring anyone into the presence of God. Before I knew it, I was in tears. I didn't realize how badly the situation as a teenager had affected me. In fact, I did not realize that I questioned and doubted the gift of music that God had given me.

That one bad experience, created a crack of hurt so deep, that it almost killed my desire for praise and worship. I was awful as a teenager after my mom died because I had a cold heart. I was so busy trying to protect myself from hurt that I did not realize how much I had hurt others. The condemnation from what my family believed about my qualification to lead had impacted me negatively. This condemnation led me on a 15-year road of struggling with the confidence to lead others into worship. I would constantly wonder if I sounded good, if I was over singing, or even qualified to lead worship. I began to compare myself to my mother feeling as if I would never be able to minister like her. I completely lost focus on the fact that worship is between you and God and as a worship leader, you just invite others to view your relationship with God through song.

After struggling with this for years, God really dealt with my heart and asked me why I valued the opinions of others over His opinion of me. In fact, why was I allowing a past moment of hurt to deter me from birthing the ministry gift that He placed inside of me? After crying hysterically because I was so broken, I realized that this situation represented a huge crack in my belief. I was struggling to trust God with my gift because I did not believe I was good enough to be a leader. I had accepted the lie that the gift of music inside of me was not good enough for God to use.

I realized that God never uses qualified people to do His work. In fact, God uses unqualified people to do His work because He wants to show others the power of transformation. It does not matter what someone thinks about my ability to sing and worship God because God qualified me to operate in this gift when He gave it to me. I had to realize that I will never be good enough at anything, but when I am weak, the God in me is strong. Whatever I lack, He fills in. Whatever I do not have, He provides because He loves me. Learning this helped me to get to where I am today, which is having the opportunity to lead worship in front of millions. God took little Alicia and made her great for His glory. Now, every time I step on a pulpit to minister, I am reminded that Jesus qualified me for that position. He trusts me with the massive gift of leading His people closer to Him. Now, what if I had allowed that one crack in my faith to hinder me from developing?

Cracks in our faith or beliefs are caused by lies. The Devil is really focused on creating a lie that seems like the truth to make it more believable. The truth is that when I sang that solo as a teenager, I probably did sound horrible but the enemy used that experience to get me to stop singing. Breaches in our faith foundation are designed to get us to stop whatever it is that we are doing that is a part of our destiny. My ability to sing has nothing to do with me, but it has everything to do with God. The moment I stepped into magnifying my skill or ability in singing was the moment I allowed a crack or breach in my belief system.

Isn't it amazing how one lie from your past can destroy your future if you allow it to? I almost stopped singing altogether because I was embarrassed from that one experience. And, guess what, there have been a million and one times where I messed up a song, forgot the words or the correct notes, but God only needed my willingness to allow Him to develop the gift in me. God just needed me to submit my gift of singing to Him for His glory, not for my own validation as a singer.

Realizing the Attack

When we doubt what God has said about us, we strengthen the lies of the enemy. The Devil works daily to get you to question who God is, what God said, and what God promised. His whole purpose is to suggest "thought darts," which are intended to simply get you to question what God has said. If the enemy can get you to question what God has said, he can form a crack in your belief. So, he throws darts of lies at your mind daily to see which one will infiltrate your faith.

Once he gets the thought in your mind, then he waits for you to say it out of your mouth. When you speak a lie out of your mouth, it becomes reality. Our words have power, so if you speak that you are a failure, it will not be long before you really are a failure. As believers, we must remember that it is Satan's job to taint or pollute the Word of God.

Sometimes, we are angry at God because we do not see the full manifestation of His Word and promises in our lives. Sometimes, it seems like God will not give you an answer or assistance in your time of need. On the other hand, unbelief or the questioning of God's Word hinders the flow of God's grace, mercy, and blessings in our lives. When we discount what God has previously done in our lives and assume that He will not do what He said He would do in our lives, we block God's ability to provide what we need. In this process, unbelief or doubt robs us of God's unlimited promises and blessings for our lives. If we are not careful, we can wind up blaming God for a lie we received from the enemy.

Since God's promises are truly available, and His Word says He will withhold no good thing from you, why would He really withhold a good thing from you? The answer is that He will not withhold any good thing from you. The truth is that if we are not seeing the full manifestation of God in our lives, there is a blockage in our faith, in our beliefs, and in our minds. Once we find the lie and eliminate it, we can move on free to experience the complete abundance that Jesus promised.

Our fight in faith is a constant battle. Different situations will arise in our lives that cause us to question the validity and truth of God's Word and promises. Unfortunately, we are met with new challenges in faith daily, but when you make a decision to trust God only, you eliminate cracks in your faith. Only considering God's Word in your life and in your situation is the key to breakthrough. Remember, the enemy wants to create cracks in your foundation of faith and belief so that he can eventually fracture your faith. One crack is all the enemy needs to go after the full foundation of what you believe is true. He ultimately seeks to fracture your faith until it is completely dismantled. In the next chapter, we will examine what happens when your faith is broken or fractured.

Chapter Summary

Believing God only is the key to eliminating cracks of unbelief. Throughout our lives, we will encounter situations that cause us to question God, His will, and His timing. In those moments, our responses should be to focus on completely trusting God. After all—has God ever really failed us? When experiencing doubt, fear, loss, hurt, rejection, bitterness, frustration, or anger, ask yourself—"What lie have I believed about this situation that may be untrue." God promises that He will never leave or forsake you. God is bound to His promises, and He is faithful to perform everything that He told you He would in your life.

Study Scriptures

"Now faith is the assurance (title deed, confirmation) of things hoped for (divinely guaranteed), and the evidence of things not seen [the conviction of their reality—faith comprehends as fact what cannot be experienced by the physical senses]."

Hebrews 11:1 (AMP)

"For we walk by faith, not by sight [living our lives in a manner consistent with our confident belief in God's promises]."

2 Corinthians 5:7 (AMP)

CHAPTER 3

Fractured Faith

"Faith was never meant to be broken."

Faith is the substance of things hoped for and the evidence of things not seen. But when we analyze faith, what is it really? Is faith just believing what God says or is faith walking in the authority that what you've asked God for is already done? I choose the second answer. Without faith, it is impossible to please God. Why? Because faith is the gateway for the manifestation of God's promises in our lives.

What is Fractured Faith?

Fractured faith occurs when a crack in our belief system has broken our trust, reliance, and faith in God. When we allow unbelief to infiltrate our minds, we give the Devil an opportunity to influence our belief system. When we question God's Word or who He is, we create the framework for a fracture in our faith. Just like a fracture in a bone, a fracture in our faith puts stress on a particular area, causing it to break and in some cases, shatter.

Faith is a weapon given to us by God to fight the fiery darts of the enemy. If it is broken or fractured, what we believe becomes shaky and unstable. In real life, a fracture can take several months to heal. Whereas, a fracture in your faith can keep you dormant and stagnant for years. When we look at the habitual cycles in our lives, more than likely, the cause is a fracture in faith. Cycles indicate that we are doing the same things, the same way, expecting a different result. Unfortunately, this process only yields insanity and chaos.

When we find ourselves waiting on God to manifest something in our lives that has not happened yet, we can become weary or tired. The most common reason for a fracture in our faith is the length of the wait associated with what we are believing God for. Initially, when God shows us a vision of our lives, it is exciting, invigorating, and life-changing. This excitement stays until we realize that there is a process that we have to go through to get to the manifestation of the vision. During this time, the enemy is on the sidelines whispering thoughts of fear and doubt aiming to influence us to quit or to even question what God said or promised. In fact, he will even place others around us who seem to be winning and getting results in their lives while we appear to be losing in life. So, what do you do when it looks like God has not provided for you? What do you do when it seems like you're in the same place, but others have advanced ahead of you?

Moses and Fractured Faith

In Exodus 3, God gives Moses a vision. He tells him that He has seen the suffering and the affliction of His people, and He gives Moses a mission or assignment to go to Pharaoh and to free His children. God gives Moses the vision, but He does not inform him about the process he will have to go through in order to see the children of Israel freed from slavery.

If you continue reading the story in Exodus, you will find that God gave Moses everything he needed to fulfill God's plan for his life on the same day He gave him that vision. In fact, the biggest battle that Moses would face was believing in his mind that he already possessed everything he needed in order to accomplish what God showed him. Every time Moses needed God, God showed up and delivered him. This was evidence that God was trustworthy. However, every time Moses encountered a new challenge in his faith, God had to remind him repeatedly that He was with him. God never gave Moses the details of how much he would have to conquer in order to get to the promised land, but he did make provision for every step of the way.

When God challenges us to grow in a new arena of faith, He may withhold answers or information to get us to grow to a new level. When God withholds details, it is for our benefit and for His glory. God leaves out important information because He knows we will quit or run if we really knew what He was grooming us for in life. The evolution of faith will always be a continuous process. There is always a greater level in faith and trust for us to achieve. The

31

situations we encounter may change, but God's Word will never change. When we question God's will or how God will provide, we unknowingly fracture our faith. Fractures create brokenness, and brokenness prevents us from functioning the way we were created and designed to live by God.

Faith requires us as believers to keep our focus solely on Jesus. If you have doubts or fears, release them to Him. If you have concerns or worries, release them to Jesus. Whatever it may be, you have to be confident that God can handle it and that He will handle it. If God showed Moses His complete plan for his life up front, I am sure he would have run away. If God presented to him all the pain and suffering he would have to endure just to free the children of Israel, I am almost certain that he would have told God He picked the wrong man for the job.

Fractured Faith and Time

Time is of the essence. Our whole society and the world move by time. Every day, we put off pursuing the vision and gifts in our hearts from God is a day wasted that we cannot get back. In the Bible, it states that the enemy comes to steal. He comes to take possession of your purpose, dreams, goals, and most of all, your time. If the Devil can get you to stall on your dream, he can prevent the dream God gave you from impacting your life and the lives of others. If the Devil can get you to stay stagnated and stuck in life cycles, he can keep you in the same place for years with no growth or development.

You would be surprised at the amount of people

who have been in the same place spiritually, mentally, and emotionally for years all because they allowed the enemy to puncture their faith and steal their time. When I reflect on my life, I realize there were several situations that I stayed in for years because I did not understand that I was in a trap. For years, after my parents' deaths, I was depressed, which means I was completely stagnant in life. When I look back, I think of all the time I wasted that I could have been writing books or traveling the world. But, in those moments, I allowed the enemy to steal my time. If these problems were dealt with quickly, I would have remained in the same depressive cycles for life.

The Delay of Time

Another aspect of time is when God makes us wait for the manifestation of His Word. The enemy knows that we want instant results in our lives and so, the concept of waiting can often deter us in our faith. It is important to note that God is not like people. God is dependable and if He promised you to do something, He must perform it because He is bound by His word. Just because God does not show up when you want Him to show up does not mean that He won't ever show up.

A delay in time is not a rejection. In moments of testing, it may look like God will never come through, but those moments are opportunities to exercise your faith. Faith solely looks at the finished works of Jesus Christ and what He has promised to us through His Word. When you are believing God for something, and it has not yet manifested, you have to realize that in God's timing what you have asked for is already done. No matter how delayed the answers you need are in your reality, faith says it is already done. The wait is not for God to do what you've asked, the wait is for the earth realm to catch up and manifest what God has already done.

Fractures Paralyze Movement

Fractures in our faith make us immobile in our beliefs and prevent us from growing in life. Sometimes, we do not yield the desired results in our lives because we have limited God in our own faith. When we use past experiences that hurt us to determine God's faithfulness to us in the future, we limit His ability in our lives. God is a creator, not an administrator. He will never just administratively run your life. While we are looking for an answer, God is creating an answer. If we limit who He is in our lives, we will never truly receive what we have asked for in prayer.

Life has a way of presenting obstacles that seem to knock the very wind and life out of you, leaving you stuck. Problems and circumstances hit you so hard, you may doubt you will even survive. Situations arise that you weren't prepared for and certainly didn't feel equipped to handle. Life is life, but God is God. Even though there are situations in our lives that leave us speechless, we have to be confident that God will perfect everything that concerns us. He may not fix it the way we want it fixed or things may get worse but just because your situation gets worse, does that truly limit who God is in your life and what He can do?

What Faith Is

Faith is never solidified in your ability to do anything. In fact, God doesn't need your ability, but what He does need is your complete reliance and trust in Him. Your faith should always be in God's ability over your own. It should be focused on the fact that Jesus Christ provided everything we would ever need when He died on the cross over 2,000 years ago. Healing, provision, love, comfort, wholeness, strategy, wisdom, faith, mercy, and grace have all been made available to us without restraint. When you believe this in your heart, you realize that faith is looking at your circumstances or problems through the lens of Jesus Christ as already solved.

When we focus on the problem more than the problem solver, we magnify the hopelessness and frustration of the situation. Whatever we choose to focus on in our minds is automatically magnified to the extent where it becomes our only focus. We may be unable to see what God is truly doing in our lives because we are so focused on the one thing that does not seem right.

Healing the Fracture

My faith became stronger when I eliminated the question of "what if?" out of my vocabulary and when I solely focused on Jesus. When I focused on the problem, I became engulfed in the problem, but when I focused on Jesus, I increased His presence in my life. Focusing on Jesus eliminates the fear of the unknown by reminding me that nothing that I do is in my own strength or ability. Everything I do is through His power, His anointing, and His unmerited favor towards me.

God does not want us dwelling on the negative things in our lives. Once we have identified an issue of concern for us, it is our job to immediately cast the care on God and seek the wisdom of Christ regarding the situation. I learned that if I focus on my past, I will become a slave in bondage to my past, unable to move into the promises of the future. Focusing on all the losses I had experienced in life was draining and limiting me. I was unable to see the good in my life because I was focused on the bad. My mind was in the wrong place. How could I believe God for a future if I was living in my past?

Whenever our faith is under stress, it can seem unbearable. We have to remind ourselves, that the faith battle is a war between what God promised and what we see. The only way to win the war is to believe and focus on what God has said more than what we do not see. These are the moments when we have to choose to activate our faith in God and choose to believe God over our present situation. Satan is real and he desires to infiltrate your belief system any way possible. If he can get access to your mind on any level, he can plant thoughts and ideas of doubt that work together to destabilize and break your faith. God is not wasteful in His pursuit of you. What may look like the end of your story, may actually just be the end of a life chapter. When we refuse to believe, we keep ourselves in bondage to our disappointments and unbelief. Having active faith means that we choose to believe that God is able to fix any situation. He is able to bring you out of whatever hopeless situations you may be facing today. Make a choice to believe God and believe God only.

Chapter Summary

We eliminate fractures in our faith when we choose to solely rely on Jesus. We have an enemy who is actively seeking opportunities to infiltrate our minds with doubt, fear, and unbelief, but faith serves as a weapon against every lie the enemy throws at us. In life, we will encounter situations that cause us to question God's Word, His timing, and His promises, but in those moments, we must settle on a faith-only attitude. God is bigger than any past, present, or future situation we may encounter in life. Though his timing is not always when we want it, it always comes when we need it.

Study Scriptures

"For this reason I am telling you, whatever things you ask for in prayer [in accordance with God's will], believe [with confident trust] that you have received them, and they will be given to you."

Mark 11:24 (AMP)

"He answered, 'Because of your little faith [your lack of trust and confidence in the power of God]; for I assure you and most solemnly say to you, if you have [living] faith the size of a mustard seed, you will say to this mountain, "Move from here to there," and [if it is God's will] it will move; and nothing will be impossible for you.'"

Matthew 17:20 (AMP)

CHAPTER 4

Broken Dreams

"If we abort our dreams, we abort our process. If we abort our process, we destroy our purpose."

When God gives you a dream, He never shows you the process of achieving that dream. He knows that if He shows you the process, your fear will prevent you from pursuing His plans for your life. Often, the dreams God places in our hearts seem and feel impossible. In fact, the bigger the dream, the bigger the impossibility of achieving the dream. God gives us dreams that seem impossible, so that when we achieve our dreams, we know that it was not in our own strength. In those moments, we recognize that God deserves the glory for making the impossible possible.

When I was a little girl, I stuttered horribly. I went to speech therapy, and it seemed like nothing was working. In my teenage years, my speech got worse. The teacher would always call on me to read, and the class would laugh because I would get stuck on words for minutes. In my mind, I told myself I would never be a speaker or a teacher. I thought I would find a nice desk job and keep to myself, but obviously, God had other plans.

As a child, every now and then, God would show me dreams of me speaking. In my mind, I would say "That's impossible!" I knew that I would never volunteer to speak out loud. Even though God showed me the dream of me speaking on pulpits and stages, I didn't believe it. The concept of me speaking was a broken idea to me. I would push it into the back of my mind thinking I was crazy. I didn't see how I would ever desire to talk in front of people in the future when I hated talking period.

My fear of speaking paralyzed me, literally. I would be filled with anxiety when someone spoke to me, and it required a response. I felt stupid before I even answered. I often thought about what others must think about me. I was embarrassed by my stuttering. When people spoke clearly and articulately, I would marvel at how easy their words slipped off their tongues. Nevertheless, God kept showing me visions of me talking and speaking around the world. And, I would just laugh in my head, condescendingly saying, "that will never happen."

Finally, I decided to take the focus off my talking challenges. I realized that if God could use Moses, who stuttered then maybe, He could use me too. I started to just say the name of Jesus when I felt myself getting stuck on a word. I began to practice reading out loud. I shifted the focus off me and my ability and began focusing on Jesus and His ability. I found that focusing on Jesus, took the focus off what I felt I couldn't do myself.

To my surprise, I graduated with a Bachelor of Arts in Journalism with a minor in public and political communication. I couldn't believe it. I graduated with a degree in a subject area that focused on me talking. The dream that I thought was impossible, was now possible. On top of that, I went on to get a Master's Degree in Teaching, which involved me talking every day to middle schoolers. When I look back now, the very idea of speaking was a broken dream to me. I didn't understand the process and how it prepared me for an even greater assignment.

Learning how to trust God in this area of my life taught me three things. First, I learned to never focus on my ability. My job is to just be obedient to God's will. I have to trust in His ability to surface every gift and skill I need to do what He has called me to do. Secondly, I learned the power of the name of Jesus. At the name of Jesus, my speech impediment had to submit to God's purpose for my life. Thirdly, I learned that when God gives you a dream or vision, it may appear broken or unfixable. In summary, stuttering was a broken area for me that caused me to doubt the validity of what God showed me as a child. Through brokenness, submission, and obedience, God taught me to never rely on myself or my own strength. My strength is in Christ. My belief in God's power and sovereignty over my speech equipped me with the strength to overcome that disability.

God Dreams

When God gives you a dream or a vision, you need faith to bring it to pass in your life. It is not just your dream, it is a "God Dream." When God plants the seed of a vision in your mind or heart, it was conceived first in God's heart. God created the dream and then, He placed it in your heart. God dreams require only obedience because God wants to fulfill the dream. In fact, God is happy when we achieve our goals in Him. It brings Him great delight and joy to see His children prospering in life.

Without complete trust and faith in God, you will never see the full manifestation of what God showed you. In our world, the cemetery is the richest place in the world because of all the people buried who died with a dream they never accomplished. Everyone has a dream or a goal, but few actually live to see it happen because doubt, fear or unbelief hindered its progress.

We, as believers, often prematurely abort our dreams because we see them as impossible. If we have no faith, we have no belief. Without belief, nothing seems possible.

Guard Your Dreams

I've always known that I was a writer. I used to write plays and poetry when I was younger. My teachers would always speak about my creativity and my gift in writing. I thought they were trying to make me feel good about myself since I had such trouble speaking. So, I didn't really believe them. Nevertheless, as I continued writing, God built my confidence in writing from His heart, and I started to believe that there was an anointing on my life to write.

So, I started a blog called *Turquoise Note,* and I began writing online. I wanted to encourage people, so I started writing on topics I thought they would want to read about. Topics like "God loves you!" and "Don't give up on God!" you know, the common cliche sermons we often hear in church. Well, to my surprise, no one read my blogs. My friends would read them to help me feel good but no one was interested.

I was so disappointed, and I almost quit, until one day God spoke to me and said: "Write transparently!" I had no idea what that meant, but I kept it in the back of my mind. One day, I was on social media and people were talking about my pastors. I was so upset and angry because the things they were saying were untrue. I wanted to defend them, but God convicted me and told me to write from a perspective of love. Many times, when people judge you, they do not have a full understanding of who you are, what you are called to, and why you may make certain decisions. These people were quick to judge my leaders, and I wanted to show God's heart. So, I wrote a blog, and it went viral. Within 24 hours, I had over 100,000 reads, multiple shares, and a full log of comments. With that one blog, God showed me my significance in His kingdom. If one little black girl like me could impact the minds of 100,000 people, what else could God use me for?

After having that successful blog post, I continued writing. My audience went down tremendously and I became discouraged. I went from having 100,000 readers to 18. I began to doubt what I was called to do. Plus, writing transparently means being vulnerable with an audience you don't know. My family began to question my activities on social media and whether it was positive for me, and I got off social media completely. I stopped blogging, I stopped writing encouraging posts, I deactivated my accounts and went back to the normal life of a teacher. Although God had shown me the vision that I would write books and novels, I decided to give up because it seemed like no one wanted to read what I had to say.

During those two months, I had a lot of time to think. I questioned why I began writing in the first place and if it was really what God called me to do, without realizing that at some point, something had transpired in my faith that changed the trajectory of my writing. Somewhere, I had believed the lies that "my writing was not good enough," "no one was reading," and "I was just another blogger clogging up the internet." Well, those were the thoughts that initially led to cracks in my belief about what God purposed for me to do. What began as a simple thought had now evolved into a mindset that led me to actually stop writing. I had stopped believing in the gift God had given me because I was consumed by the lack of participation and support I gave up on my vision because I did not see the provision for the vision.

The "weight of the opinions of others" began to "outweigh" the weight of the word God had given me. The innocent criticisms of family and friends regarding my writing had now become enough to solidify why I should not be writing. I had allowed the weight of their words to become greater than my purpose and passion. And, I found myself in the process of prematurely aborting the dream that God placed inside of me, which was the enemy's plan all along.

I did not realize that the enemy is a dream killer. He will do whatever it takes to get you to give up on the dreams and vision that God has placed in your heart because he is a thief. I did not know that I had to "guard my dreams."

The Story of Joseph

In Genesis 37, we are introduced to the main character, Joseph. In my mind, I imagine Joseph was handsome, multi-talented, and anointed by God. He was favored by his father, and his brothers hated him for it. Israel, his father gave him a beautiful coat filled with many colors, so that people would be aware of his presence and know of his favor, but, his brothers hated him more because of this.

One day, Joseph dreamed a "God dream," a dream that was given solely to him by God Himself. He was so confident in his dream; he told his brothers about it and how he would rule over them one day. Immediately, his brothers were filled with passionate hatred and conspired to kill him. Then, Joseph had another dream about him ruling over many, and he shared it with his brothers. Well, this dream fueled their envy and jealousy of Joseph, and they conspired to kill him.

Genesis 37: 18 - 24 (Amplified)

18 And when they saw him from a distance, even before he came close to them, they plotted to kill him. 19 They said to one another, "Look, here comes this dreamer. 20 Now then, come and let us kill him and throw him into one of the pits (cisterns, underground water storage); then we will say [to our father], 'A wild animal killed and devoured him'; and we shall see what will become of his dreams!" 21 Now Reuben [the eldest] heard this and rescued him from their hands and said, "Let us not take his life." 22 Reuben said to them, "Do not shed his blood, but [instead] throw him [alive] into the pit that is here in the wilderness, and do not lay a hand on him [to kill him]"—[he said this so] that he could rescue him from them and return him [safely] to his father. 23 Now when Joseph reached his brothers, they stripped him of his tunic, the [distinctive] multicolored tunic which he was wearing; 24 then they took him and threw him into the pit. Now the pit was empty; there was no water in it.

Can you imagine how much his brothers must have hated him to conspire to kill him? When Joseph shared his dreams, I do not believe his intent was to boast to his brothers. I believe he was confident in what God showed him, to the point where he was willing to share with others not knowing that this would cause his brothers to put him in a pit, and leave him for dead.

Fortunately, his brother, Judah convinced his brothers not to kill him but to sell him into slavery. Judah knew that if Joseph was really anointed by God, he didn't want Joseph's blood to be on his hands. So, he convinced his brothers to let Joseph live, and he was sold as a slave. From this story, we learn that although we want others to believe in our dreams, everyone will not always have the foresight or the heart to see where God is taking us. When Joseph shared his vision, he did not expect to immediately come under attack for simply voicing what God showed him. Like many of us, he simply shared his dream prematurely.

God requires us to guard our dreams. We cannot tell everyone our visions because they are the visions God placed in our hearts, not theirs. When we share our visions prematurely, we open ourselves to the influence of the enemy. We open the door to criticism and worldly wisdom that will destroy the original intent or purpose of God's Word for our lives.

The story of Joseph is a great example of how God gave him the vision but did not show him the process to accomplishing the vision. Joseph saw that he would be a ruler over many, but he didn't see all the things he would have to overcome to be a ruler over many.

If you continue reading the story of Joseph in Genesis 39, you will find that God was with him through every trial he experienced. Ironically, it was the sharing of his dream with his brothers that started Joseph on the road to his destiny.

The day that Joseph was thrown into the pit, I

am sure he thought to himself that his dream was over. God showed him that he was a great leader, but now he was a slave. God showed him that his brothers would bow before him, but now he was in a foreign land with his whereabouts unknown to his family. Joseph's situation looked the opposite of what God promised him, but this was a deception. It is important to note that our sight will often deceive us. Just because we do not see what we need, does not mean it is not available to us. When our dreams look like they are broken and disfigured, God is not moved. God is able to turn a mess into a message at any moment.

God was with Joseph throughout all his trials. God kept His promise and favored him even in the worst of situations. Joseph innocently endured years of slavery and imprisonment, but God used these situations to work on his heart. Sometimes, God will allow our dreams to seem broken so that He can work on our hearts.

During Joseph's time in jail and slavery, God developed forgiveness, love, compassion, grace, and peace in him. He used what the enemy originally planned for evil and made it good. Although the vision may have looked unobtainable, Joseph eventually walked into everything God showed him.

The thing with dreams is that when God makes a large investment in you, He will grow His investment until it is ready to harvest. God invested into Joseph and He was not going to allow Joseph to die in that pit. God already had a plan to take care of Joseph and to teach him everything he needed to know about the attributes and character of a good leader.

If God has given you a vision, it is because He trusts you with it. On the other hand, before God gives you the dream, he needs to know that you are adequately prepared in wisdom and humility to handle everything He is going to give you.

When Dreams Seem Broken

When failure is involved in our dreams, we give up. Correspondingly, we begin to believe that a "failing" makes us a "failure." In reality, however, some of the most successful people in this world experienced many "failings," and were never "failures." Just because you failed at something does not mean you are a failure. Just because it looks like you are going in the opposite direction in life, does not mean that God doesn't have a plan for everything you are going through. You have to believe that God does not design us to fail. And if you feel like you have failed that just means that "God is not finished with the plot of your story."

The biggest question and decision you will ever make in life is whether you should quit or continue? The enemy is not after you or your family. He is after your dream, which is directly correlated to your purpose. If he can steal your dream, he can abort your purpose. And if he can abort your purpose, he can wipe out the very reason God created you.

Disappointments will happen in life, but God's love for us is consistent and unchanging. What looks like the end of something, may be the beginning of a new area. If you hold onto what's broken, you can never receive what is whole. Your dreams cannot be tied to someone else's success. Your decision to be confident and bold about who God has called you to be is a decision that will impact someone's life.

When we experience brokenness in our dreams, it gives God an opportunity to be God in our lives. When we are vulnerable in His presence, fully aware of our wounds and disappointments, we allow the presence of God to bind up and heal those wounds. I never thought I would heal from the hurt and pain of my parents' deaths. I didn't think it was possible to move on through life without them. There were moments when their absence rang loudly in my ears. Moments when I cried desperately with tears creating rivers of pain down my cheeks. But, in all of my hurt and in all of my brokenness, I surrendered to God.

Perhaps, you are not where you want to be in life. I know the disappointment of an unfulfilled dream is difficult but the beauty of God's ability to heal that wound is greater. Perhaps, you are waiting on a spouse, and it seems like nothing is happening in your dating life. That dream of marriage may be broken for you, but God can fix it. You may be believing God for a child, and it seems like everyone around you is having children, but God can fix it.

When it seems like our dreams have failed, we have to realize that healing comes through the acceptance that Jesus is greater than our "failures." There is nothing that God cannot fix or revive, especially if it is a dream He placed in our hearts.

Refusing to Abort the Process

When we abort our dreams prematurely, we give up on our partnership with God. God is not looking for you to find a way to make the dream happen, He is looking for you to have faith in Him to bring the dream to fruition. God Dreams require our faith. God needs us to believe in His word for our lives even if others do not understand or accept it. God does not want you pursuing your dreams without Him, He wants you to include Him. He desires you to seek His will, His plan, His methods, His strategies, His provision, and every other aspect of wisdom that you will need.

If your dream has not happened or if you have endured a great loss, it does not mean that God does not have greater for you. God's Word tells us that God will withhold no good thing. We are the sole-heirs of Christ. We were created to walk in purpose and have abundant life in Him. We were created to win. We were created to succeed. We were created to walk in purpose and live abundantly. We are not cowards. We are not quitters. We are God's children, and we have a purpose. God knew of all your failures, hurts, life experiences, losses, and brokenness before you even existed, and still trusted you with His dream. You are chosen. Don't abort the process. Dream again with God.

Do not allow discouragement to cloud the possibility of the future in your life. You may have a lot of bills but not enough money, however, God showed you a financially abundant life. Keep that vision before you. Do not be swayed or moved by the debt or bills that you see. It may seem like you are moving backward, but God can easily reroute your direction. Joseph looked like he was moving in the opposite direction of what God showed him, but he was actually progressing toward the goal.

Backward is not always backward with Jesus. Jesus can take what looks backward and use it to make us progress further. What looks like a setback is often a step in the right direction. Trust God with your process and allow your dream to become a reality.

Chapter Summary

When God gives us a dream, He requires our faith. We do not place our faith in the dream, but we place our faith in His ability to fulfill the dream. When we take the focus off ourselves and shift it onto Jesus, we eliminate the concept of failure in our lives. Dreams can only be broken when we insert our cares, our worries, and our weights from life into them. If God gave you a dream, it is because He trusts you with it. Believe only.

Study Scriptures

"It shall come about after this that I shall pour out My Spirit on all mankind; And your sons and your daughters will prophesy, Your old men will dream dreams, Your young men will see visions."

Joel 2:28 (AMP)

"I can do all things [which He has called me to do] through Him who strengthens and empowers me [to fulfill His purpose—I am self-sufficient in Christ's sufficiency; I am ready for anything and equal to anything through Him who infuses me with inner strength and confident peace.]"

Philippians 4:13 (AMP)

CHAPTER 5

The Leverage of Dirty Secrets

"When we hide secrets, we invite immobility into our spiritual lives."

Secrets are the things we keep hidden in our hearts and minds hoping that no one will ever know or discover the truth. Secrets provide leverage for the enemy to attack us spiritually, mentally, emotionally, and physically. The weight and depth of a secret can seem better hidden, but often, it creates in-roads for the enemy to condemn us in our faith and beliefs.

The first secret ever established was in the Garden of Eden. After partaking of the forbidden fruit, Adam and Eve saw it fit to hide in fear of what God would say and do when He discovered their disobedience. Before that, they had no fear. Fear was introduced after they disobeyed God. Fear entered when they became afraid of the consequences of their choices.

Genesis 3: 1 - 3 (Amplified)

3 Now the serpent was more crafty (subtle, skilled in deceit) than any living creature of the field which the Lord God had made. And the serpent (Satan) said to the woman, "Can it really be that God has said, 'You shall not eat from any tree of the garden'?" 2 And the woman said to the serpent, "We may eat fruit from the trees of the garden, 3 except the fruit from the tree which is in the middle of the garden. God said, 'You shall not eat from it nor touch it, otherwise you will die.'

In the scripture reference above, we see that the serpent captured the attention of Eve by getting her to question God's omniscience—His ability to know all things. He got Eve to question the sovereignty of God's authority by simply suggesting that God was withholding something from her and Adam. Eve accepted this thought, which later led her to eat from the forbidden tree.

The enemy's strategy is always to get us to question whether God is withholding something from us. We all have dreams, desires, and goals, but what happens when we begin to question if God has forgotten us, or if He does not trust us? What happens when we begin to question if God has lied to us concerning something He said?

Well, what happens is we give the enemy an open door to establish distrust in our relationship with God. When Eve was speaking with the serpent, she was aware of what God had told Adam concerning what they could and could not eat. When Eve began to question God's authority, she gave the enemy permission to establish a root of unbelief in her heart.

When we question God's word concerning our lives, we give an open invitation to doubt and unbelief. We immediately begin to doubt if God will really do what He said He will do and if He is withholding something from us.

Genesis 3: 4 - 5 (Amplified)

But the serpent said to the woman, "You certainly will not die! 5 For God knows that on the day you eat from it your eyes will be opened [that is, you will have greater awareness], and you will be like God, knowing [the difference between] good and evil."

After the serpent successfully tricked Eve into questioning the validity of God's word, he then appealed to her self-centeredness. In verse 5, the enemy told Eve that she would have greater awareness and that she would be like God. Well, that was an absolute lie. Adam and Eve were already like God but the moment Eve believed the serpent, unbelief took root in her heart.

Whether you know it or not, the root of every sin is pride. Out of the desire to protect ourselves, we often do whatever is necessary. The moment the enemy gets us to step into pride is the moment we become like him. Satan's biggest sin was not his betrayal of God, but it was his desire to think that he was like God, which is pride. When what we think becomes greater than what God has said, we step into pride. Meaning, we begin to trust ourselves over the word of God.

If you continue reading the story, you find that after eating the forbidden fruit, Adam and Eve immediately hid. In their desire to keep their previous actions a secret, they began to hide from God. This is interesting because when we sin, the first thing we do is hide. As if God does not already know what we just did. In our own pride, we think that hiding the issue protects us, when in reality, it just condemns us. It is important to note that the same enemy who will entice you to sin is the same enemy who will condemn you after you sin.

When I was a teenager, I was an avid liar. I would often lie because I was afraid of what would happen if someone knew the truth. Unfortunately, the decision to lie kept me in bondage because I had to maintain my truth of the lie. When we hide things from God, we prevent true healing and restoration from taking place in our lives. When I was afraid to tell people that my parents died from AIDS, I kept myself in bondage to my past. In other words, when we hold onto secrets in our lives, we invite shame and bitterness into our hearts.

The Root of a Secret

The enemy is always looking for a way to distract you, trap you, and eternally damn you to hell. Sometimes, we forget that the source of all evil is Satan himself. In today's society, it is easy to get caught up in politics, race issues, gun control issues, and a plethora of significant issues that plague our world. Furthermore, the source of all evil is the Devil. God is a God of love, and Satan is the creator of division, chaos, and frustration.

For a long time, the secret I was ashamed of was my parents. Deciding to disclose that my father was involved an extramarital affair with a priest was not the most exciting news to share. Nevertheless, over time, I realized that the enemy could only shame me if I was unwilling to expose it myself.

When we carry and harbor secrets, we are unwilling to allow God to heal the true root of the problems that occurred in our lives. By not talking about the death of my parents and how it affected me as a young woman, I only embraced the theology that I had to carry the weight of my past.

How often do we carry the weight of our past because we are unwilling to be truly authentic with God? How often do we carry secrets because we assume others are too weak to handle the truth? How many times do we keep our mouths closed because we think we are doing God a favor?

You may not know the answers to these questions or perhaps you do. The reality is that in order to be free, we must live transparently. Being transparent means you are willing to expose anything of your past if God asks you to do it. As a young woman, I had to be willing to allow God to take my story and use it to impact the lives of others.

Although it is absolutely horrible how my parents came to their death, the beauty is that sharing their story helps and heals so many other families that may be experiencing similar situations. Amazingly, God can use our dirty secrets to help set someone else free from bondage.

When we examine the root or foundation of a secret, the base is self-centeredness or pride. We feel that we must keep the family name sacred or hold the respect and honor of ourselves or others. Perhaps, telling the secret may damage the persona and reputation that we have worked so hard to build. While on the contrary, acknowledging the truth will always set us free mentally, spiritually, and emotionally.

My family and friends did not know how to appropriately talk about what transpired between my mother and father. This caused me to speculate all kinds of stories in my head to explain their relationship. When I finally learned the truth, the weight of the situation lifted off of me. I no longer had to assume. What happened between them and what had been a dirty secret was now exposed as truth. This provided me with closure and healing.

God could care less about your secrets, but He does care about your willingness to allow Him to expose the truth in your life. God is not looking for someone to have a great reputation, He is looking for someone to have a pure heart. The truth will set you free—even if it is an ugly truth. You do not have to tell the world your secrets, but you can share them with those whose lives can be healed by them.

Living in Transparency

When we accept Jesus Christ into our lives, we sign up for a life of transparency. Deciding to give God everything in our hearts, minds, bodies and souls is the foundation for supernatural transformation and breakthrough. Secrets are designed to kill your development and growth. If we are unwilling to expose the dirty secrets in our lives, we willingly choose to be in bondage to the enemy. The concept of vulnerability is a prerequisite to having a successful relationship with Christ. He requires that we bring every issue before Him, not leaving out any information and putting the whole truth before Him. It is in those moments that He can correct us, encourage us, and give us the knowledge to make better choices. God wants us to lay all of our hurts, offenses, resentment, bitterness, depression, emptiness, fears, and heartache before Him, so that He can do spiritual and emotional open-heart surgery on us. God is interested in every situation in our lives. There is nothing that you can hide from Him.

Living transparently means that when people see you, they see the Christ in you. The light of Christ inside of you desires to illuminate the glory of God. God is interested in demonstrating His love, grace, and mercy to you and through you. When we bring everything in our lives to God, we give Him the opportunity to fix our situations and our hearts. Withholding information from God keeps us caged in the condemnation or fear of the situation we keep as a secret. Transparency is the gateway to deliverance.

Chapter Summary

When we harbor secrets, we prevent true healing in our lives. We may often think we are protecting our loved ones but when they are exposed to the truth, it will hurt them more if they realize we withheld information from them. Exposing the secrets in our lives forces us to take accountability for our actions, and it allows us to receive true healing. When we expose our secrets, we eliminate any leverage that the enemy may use to condemn us. God already knows our secrets and is fully equipped to deal with the issues of our hearts.

Study Scriptures

"So He said to them, 'You are the ones who declare yourselves just and upright in the sight of men, but God knows your hearts [your thoughts, your desires, your secrets]; for that which is highly esteemed among men is detestable in the sight of God.'"

Luke 16: 15 (AMP)

"Would not God discover this? For He knows the secrets of the heart."

Psalm 44:21 (AMP)

CHAPTER 6

Crevices of Hurt

"Hurt prevents us from truly trusting God."

In life, we face inevitable crevices of hurt. A crevice of hurt is a narrow opening or crack in your heart caused by extreme pain or offense by another individual. Heart situations like these force us to evaluate the depth of God's love for us. Some of us build emotional walls of protection to prevent further hurt. Others refuse to deal with the hurt, lock it away, and pretend that it never happened. And for the rest of us, we take our broken hearts to God asking Him to mend the shattered pieces of our lives. Whether we choose to admit it or not, hurt and offense provide the enemy with the tools needed to sever the intimacy of our relationship with Jesus Christ.

When we refuse to deal with the hurt in our lives, we choose to nurture and keep it. In Matthew 6:15, God commands us to forgive others because if we do not, it will negatively affect our relationship with Him. Unforgiveness is an immediate opening for the Devil to sow seeds of confusion, discourse, resentment and hatred in your heart. Dealing with extreme hurt in our lives requires us to establish our truth before God. Bringing the situation to Him as it is, not withholding any information, and placing the good, bad, and ugly of the situation before Him. Lingering in hurt and pain will keep you paralyzed in hurt and pain.

When people you love cause you pain, you have to remind yourself to love the person but dislike their actions or choices that resulted in you being hurt. It is important to know that the love of God supersedes any hurt, pain, betrayal, or disappointment that you have experienced. There is no problem, no circumstance, no addiction, no pain, no issue that we face that is bigger than the God we serve. There is never a situation that God is unprepared for in our lives. His love knows no boundaries for us. His love has no walls or limitations. In His love, we are perfected.

Hurt breeds fear. It trains the mind and heart to live carefully in fear of what could happen if you choose to love freely. However, faith is confronting that fear with nothing to protect you but Jesus Christ. When we choose to love freely, it is like jumping out of a plane, not knowing where we will land but trusting God with where we will end up.

People will always hurt us, fail us, and let us down because they are human. Sometimes, they will even do it repeatedly. Unfortunately, we all fall and we all miss the mark at some point in our lives. As a result of this, we must give our human limitations to

God because He is able to exceed our expectations in anything we ask or think.

The Crevice of Rejection

The biggest hurt I have dealt with in my life is rejection. I've always felt like I was not good enough, great enough, strong enough, pretty enough, and realistically just not enough in every area. After my parents died, my world was shattered. The people who were supposed to be there to protect me were unable to. I felt alone, and I wanted to fit in so badly. I wanted to feel love and acceptance because the world I was accepted in was now gone.

I am convinced that rejection is a primary root of suicide. Over the past few years, suicide has become a familiar road of escape for many who feel like all is lost. Countless teenagers have taken their lives because of rejection and bullying at school from peers. Adults have taken their lives because of personal failures and feeling as if those who once loved and accepted them will change because of the bad decisions they have made. Rejection is common and if not addressed properly, it can lead to a long road of depression and sorrow, ultimately causing one to linger in a crevice of hurt.

At some point in our lives, we all want to be accepted and loved. Unfortunately, some people spend their entire lives attempting to fit into a group that they never belonged in. It could be a group at work, your family or even your church family. Rejection is something we will all experience in life. Most people don't talk about it because it seems silly, but the enemy has used it to destroy people for generations.

The truth is that Satan was rejected by God when he attempted to think himself like God. For that reason, he has spent his time on earth creating the illusion that we are rejected as well. Everything the enemy throws at us is just a smokescreen of what happened to him, and the greatest deception is for us to believe we are rejected by someone or anything that doesn't have the power to reject us. Satan attempts to project his feelings of resentment and bitterness on us and if we are not careful, we will accept those feelings and emotions that distance us further from God. He uses rejection to create crevices of hurt in our hearts that cause us to examine and question God's character and heartbeat.

The issue of being accepted is important to all of us but for some, it weighs heavily on us, especially when we've experienced many losses in life. For me, the enemy always created scenarios in my life that reinforced the feelings of rejection. For example, if the people that I love mistakenly forgot to call me or invite me to an event, but called everyone else. Other times, I would be in relationships that would devalue me and affirm the notion that there was no one who would accept me for who I was.

Hurt and offense can be very painful but if we allow God to deal with them, we will overcome. It is only when we hide or refuse to deal with them, that they grow and fester into anger, bitterness, and resentment. Without realizing it when we experience hurt, we can become even more distant from those who truly love us. This process further creates the illusion that we are alone and unaccepted by those we love.

Rejection works to convince you that you are not enough and will never be enough. It convinces you that something is wrong with you and that if you could fix that one issue, things would magically be better. You may start to compare yourself to others, which breeds extreme discontentment in your own life.

The enemy will often attack you in areas that are crucial to your development in Christ. He will use issues of acceptance and hurt to distract you from moving forward in life. His ultimate goal is to attack your identity in Christ and if you do not know who you are, you will find yourself drifting along in life purposelessly.

From my experience, here are some lessons God taught me about rejection:

1. No one has the authority to accept you or reject you. You are a child of God, no one can take away your significance unless you give them the authority to.

2. Rejection often occurs when we attempt to be a part of something we were never designed to be included in. God desires for us to find our identity in Him, not in other people.

3. Jesus Christ was rejected by those He healed and prayed for when He was crucified on the cross. Jesus is sensitive to how it feels when we are unaccepted, betrayed, and lied on. Therefore, Christ is equipped to handle and

heal your heart. He was rejected, so that through Him, we could be accepted.

4. Communicate your heart to God. It is in moments of transparency with the Father, that He is able to heal the wounds of our hearts. Be honest with God and expose the wounds completely, not covering or hiding anything.

5. Forgive quickly. When Jesus was on the cross, He told the Father to forgive the people because they did not know what they were doing. When we harbor unforgiveness, we give the enemy immediate access to our hearts. Forgiveness is not for the other person; it is for you. When we practice forgiveness, we allow our lives to move forward.

6. If possible, talk with the person who has offended or hurt you. You cannot control their response, but you can control your heart towards them. If speaking with them is not an option, write a letter to them blatantly stating everything you feel. When you finish the letter, surrender everything in it to God. As a symbol of your decision to forgive, tear the letter up and move on with life.

Lastly, remember that if God can forgive us of all our sins, then who are we to hold a grudge or offense against someone else. God's love is real and His love is the only acceptance we need. When we are in bondage to people, we place those people above God and His will for our lives. Every person God used in the Bible had to be free from the opinions and criticisms of other people. God is looking for people who are obedient to Him, and Him only. When we are in bondage to people, it affects our decision-making and the ability to hear the instructions of God clearly. We can easily become confused and paralyzed in our movements toward His plans for our lives.

We will never be able to please everyone, but you can live a life free from the expectations and demands of people and society. The truth is that we are never rejected. We are children of God. We are fearfully and wonderfully made even with all of our flaws. When Jesus accepts you, it does not matter what anyone else thinks or even how they make you feel. Jesus has the final word, the final say. Therefore, we must rest in knowing that we have been accepted and adopted by God.

The Crevice of Loss

When we lose the people we love, our first thought is to question God and His sovereignty. Whether it is the loss of a loved one or a relationship, we can find ourselves questioning "Where is God?" In a world filled with sickness, disease, addictions, and other things that negatively impact relationships, it is natural for us to question why God allows certain things to happen? This question plagued me after the death of my parents. I was looking for answers concerning why I experienced so much grief early in my life. Didn't God know that I would need parents? Why didn't He stop the progression of HIV in my parents' bodies?

When we experience loss of any kind, we feel stripped of something or someone close to us who we believed was essential to our lives. The loss of a parent, the loss of a child, the loss of a job, the loss of a friendship, the loss of a marriage, and the loss of finances can cause us to question what's happening in our lives and our purpose.

Every decision we make has a consequence. We are free moral agents, which means that we have the ability to lead our lives. When we begin to question the sovereignty of God's will, we open our minds to knowledge that may be too great for us to understand or comprehend. Without the assistance of the Holy Spirit, we can stumble into knowledge without the clear revelation of how that knowledge pertains to us and our situations. God's will is never for anyone to be sick or to die, but we live in a world that is influenced by the Devil. Satan desires to kill by any means necessary.

This is why it is important that we as believers know the Word of God and the authority that God gives us. God gives us the authority to heal and to deliver; however, because we are often unaware of the power we possess, we settle for the issues life gives us. Not realizing that God's Word is fully capable of battling and winning over any sickness, disease, hurt, or loss. Through the power and name of Jesus Christ, God has given us the authority over every trap of the enemy.

Although the loss of my parents was very hard, I had to rest in the fact that they were now in heaven, where they are free of sickness, illness, disease, hurt, debt, and anything else they faced on this earth. When people die, regardless of how they died or when they died, if they have received Jesus Christ, they are in a better place. The blessing in my loss is how God uses my story to help others who have experienced similar situations. Instead of focusing on how much I lost, I started focusing on what God wanted me to gain. Being free from a crevice of loss, or a narrow-minded way of thinking that only allows you to see the negative of a situation simply means that I shifted my thinking from what I lost, to what God says I will gain.

In the Bible, Job lost everything. He lost his family, his friends, his assets, his home, and basically his life. However, he gained so much more after that process. If he had only focused on what he lost, he would never have been able to embrace what God was giving him. There have been relationships that I lost, that completely devastated me, but I realized that God had so much more in store for me. I knew that if I continued to dwell on the losses, I could never embrace the promises of God for my life.

In my experience here are some lessons God taught me about loss:

1. Be completely honest with God about how you feel. Your honesty will not scare or offend Him.

2. Find scriptures that express your thoughts or your feelings about where you are in your heart.

3. Find ways to remember the person in a positive light. Start a foundation or something that honors their memory.

4. Trust that God is able to fill your broken heart with His love. Be open to new relationships or even mentoring others who have experienced a similar loss.

5. Ask the Holy Spirit to heal every wound in your heart and allow yourself to let go. Letting go does not mean you forget the person, it simply means you let go of the hurt.

6. Whenever you miss the person or the relationship, give all the tears, frustrations, and   pain to God. Next, quote God's Word pertaining to the situation and release it into His hands.

Whenever I think of my mother and father and how much I miss them, I think of how blessed they are to be at rest in heaven. I think of how God has blessed me and how His Word in Psalms 138:8 says He will perfect everything that concerns me. It is important to know that trusting in God requires our faith even when we do not understand.

The Crevice of Pride

Any hurt or offense that we experience in life is related to our pride or self-centeredness. When we lose someone, we are upset because it affects us. When we suffer the loss of a job, we are upset because it affects us. When someone dies, we are upset because it hurts us. Regardless of what the wound is, there is a little root of selfishness somewhere.

Have you ever wondered why Jesus never took offense to the people who crucified Him? Jesus had every right to be offended after those He loved dearly betrayed Him. Can you imagine how He must have felt when the same people who praised Him and sought healing from Him were also the same people who crucified Him? Nevertheless, He never once let offense take root in His heart because he understood that offense gives the enemy an open road to come into your life. Christ understood that the ultimate gift of love is to serve others, even when they do not recognize who you are.

Jesus understood that His life was a reflection of God and not of Himself. He could have certainly chosen to take offense or be hurt by the people He loved, but His destiny was greater than the betrayal of others. At some point, as we live for Christ, we have to realize and accept that our lives do not entirely belong to us. We are witnesses. We are the light in a dark world. We are vessels that God seeks to use to demonstrate His love and truth in.

When we allow hurt or offense to take root in our hearts. We tell God that the pain is greater than His promise for our lives. We make a decision to put ourselves first instead of relinquishing control of our lives and hearts to God. In order for God to truly have access to our hearts, we must be vulnerable to Him and to others. Being vulnerable allows us to be free from any emotional distraction that would hinder our intimacy with God.

God requires us to be transparent in our relationship with Him. He requires us to be willing to let go of all our hurt and pain of the past in order for us to move into our future. Harboring unforgiveness or pride shuts down God's ability to move freely in our hearts our lives, and in our situations.

In every situation we face, God gives us a choice to trust Him or to trust ourselves. The answer to every situation we face in life is Jesus. When we make a choice to read the Word of God, speak the Word of God, and be obedient to the will of God for our lives, we leave no room for the enemy or his suggestions. If Jesus can put the will of God first, surely, we can follow in His footsteps and put the will of God first.

When You Hurt Someone

Although the bulk of this chapter is about when you have experienced hurt, I must also give wisdom to you for when you have hurt someone. Hurt people often hurt people. It is the cycle that keeps on giving until we stop it. If you have hurt someone that you love, the first step to healing is to get over your pride. The pride that says you were right to say what you said or do what you did to them. The pride that says it is okay to retaliate when it is not okay. The same forgiveness that God offers you, is the same forgiveness that you have to offer to others. Vengeance is never justified when you take it upon yourself to handle a situation or offend someone. Vengeance belongs to God, and you have to trust that He will take care of the situation perfectly, without your interference.

When you have wronged someone, you have to apologize, acknowledge where you went wrong in the situation and be completely honest. Next, you need to forgive yourself and be willing to accept the consequences of your actions. Thirdly, you must realize that you are human, and you may offend many people in your humanness but nothing is too hard for God to fix, not even you. God is faithful to solve your problem with another individual, but you must be open to His methods. Sometimes, He may require you to separate yourself from the person or situation while He works on your heart and theirs for future reconciliation. Other times, He may require you to let go of the situation while you completely trust that He has your best interest at heart. Whatever His wisdom is on how to handle the situation, be obedient to His instructions.

God does not participate in cycles. He stops them. God does not resend bad relationships and connections if He knows they will be harmful to you and other individuals. However, He does require that you completely abandon yourself in the process as you fully trust His guidance regarding the situation. When God "gifts" a relationship, whether romantic or platonic, believe that He will present you with His best.

You will never be perfect, but God's grace on your life already equips you with everything you need to handle the good, bad, and ugly situations in life. We all hurt people at some point, but once you notice a cycle, you have to let God come in and break it. Broken relationships are not God's will for your life.

Chapter Summary

Crevices of hurt, rejection, loss, and pride are avenues that prevent us from fully trusting in God. When we stay in a place of offense, we invite the enemy to sow lies into our hearts concerning God and who He is. Satan loves to play in the unresolved, unhealed, and unsealed wounds in our hearts. These things can build strongholds of fear, doubt, and unbelief, which will keep you thinking narrow-mindedly about your situation. When dealing with any type of discomfort in life, the immediate answer is to seek Jesus Christ and allow Him to mend your broken pieces. If you were the one who offended someone else, rest in God's forgiveness, knowing that He has already equipped you with everything you need to humble yourself in that situation and to show His love and compassion to the other person.

Study Scriptures

14 "For if you forgive others their trespasses [their reckless and willful sins], your heavenly Father will also forgive you. 15 But if you do not forgive others [nurturing your hurt and anger with the result that it interferes with your relationship with God], then your Father will not forgive your trespasses."

Matthew 6:14-15 (AMP)

3 "He heals the brokenhearted. And binds up their wounds [healing their pain and comforting their sorrow]."

Psalm 147:3 (AMP)

.

CHAPTER 7

Paralyzing Crevices of Fear

"In God's love, there is no room for fear."

FEAR
Fear paralyzes.
Fear kills your ideas.
Fear kills your hope.
Fear kills your expectation.
Fear destroys your belief.
Fear destroys your heart.
Fear destroys your dreams.
Fear creates unbelief.
Fear creates self-centeredness.
Fear creates illusions.
Fear blocks truth.
Fear blocks love.
Fear blocks God.

-Alicia H. Watson-

In order to fully trust in God, we must be free of fear. Being afraid of the future prevents us from moving in the present. It paralyzes us in the natural and supernatural by preventing movement, hindering growth, and blocking us from receiving from God. Fear is an enemy to your faith, your development, and your prosperity. It originates from the bad experiences you have had or seen in the lives of others. And, in an effort to prevent further bad things from happening, fear develops and overtakes your ability to truly trust God.

Push Through Your Fear

A few years ago, one of my best friends and I decided to take a trip to California. We were near the Sacramento area when we realized that Lake Tahoe was about 2 hours away. So, we decided we would drive there. As we drove, we realized the elevation level kept rising. We noticed a change in air temperature, and suddenly, we saw pieces of snow. We laughed and thought: *It's April, this cannot be real snow*, and we kept driving. Well, it was real snow and as we went higher up the mountain, we realized we could not turn around, so we had to press forward.

If we had known that we had to drive through the Sierra Nevada Mountains, we would never have decided to go to Lake Tahoe. At one point, we reached an elevation of 7,000 feet in the air, and it was scary. As we drove, you could see deep crevices in the mountain and snow-covered trees surrounding us. It was absolutely beautiful. My friend was having a panic attack and kept telling me to turn around. With this in mind, I decided that we were too far up the mountain to turn around. Well, after almost 2 hours of driving, we made it to the amazing Lake Tahoe. The view was absolutely stunning. In that moment, I realized that fear is just fear until it is conquered.

The beauty and serenity on the other side of the mountain were breathtakingly glorious. For about an hour, we walked around the lake, just taking in the thought that God could have created something so beautiful. Even though the journey had been treacherous, the canvas of God's beauty that awaited us was unexplainable.

It is important to know that fear represents the mountains in our lives. When we are afraid, we see the problem as a mountain that we will never conquer. If we do not press forward, we may never see what blessings await us on the other side. If we had turned around before reaching our destination, we would never have seen the breathtaking view of the snow-capped mountains of Sierra Nevada. If we had allowed our fear to stop us, we would have gone home experiencing nothing but a long, pointless, road trip.

Eliminating Fear

When we have fear in our lives, we must realize that our focus has shifted. When we focus on the problems in our lives, we have taken our focus off of Jesus. But, when we focus on Jesus, we make Him bigger than all of our problems. When I was driving up that mountain, I didn't focus on the ice, the snow, the rising elevation level, or the fact that there were no rails on the highway to protect us. I focused on my determination to get to Lake Tahoe. If I had considered everything that was around us, I would have turned back. But, by keeping my focus on my destination, I eliminated the fear of what surrounded me.

In life, the only consideration is Jesus. When we allow the enemy or the world to suggest anything that is contrary to the will of God, we invite fear. Fear is rooted in perception and what we perceive is danger. In reality, there is nothing to be afraid of when we are in God's will for our lives.

Fear Paralyzes

When we are consumed by fear, we are unable to move. We are stagnant and unproductive because we are afraid of what could happen to us if we step out on faith. For example, this book was in my heart for about 5 years before I actually decided to write it. I was afraid of what people would say, would it be too deep or religious, or would it even make sense. I allowed fear to prevent me from writing and even as I write, I still have the same thoughts, but I shifted my focus on Jesus and took my focus off me and my own limitations.

When I look at my limitations, fear immediately steps in. I do not know everything about the Bible, and I am continuously studying God's Word for revelation but does it mean that I am unqualified to write what God has given me? The answer is no. The world does not qualify me to write this book, but God qualifies me to do all things through Christ.

You will never be qualified for what God has called you to do. You will never have enough degrees or awards under your name that support where Jesus wants to take you in life. Fear causes you to look at yourself and what you lack, whereas faith requires that you to look at Jesus and what He has already provided for you. Fear says you do not know enough to start a business, but faith says to start a business, and I will surround you with people who have the wisdom to run a business. Fear says you will never get out of debt, but faith says Jesus already paid my debt, and He will give me strategies to eliminate them. Fear will always hinder, block, or destroy, whereas faith will always move forward, promote, or open new opportunities.

Fear will cause us to build internal walls. Walls that prevent us from exploring the unknown because of the failures or setbacks we have experienced in the past. Walls prevent us from going out and others from coming in. Internal walls also prevent God from freely distributing His grace toward us because we have locked ourselves into a safe place. Often, everything we desire in God lies outside of our walls. When we build emotional fortresses to keep people out and to protect ourselves, we are in essence telling God that we do not trust Him enough to protect us. Sometimes, extreme pain and hurt can serve as reset buttons for our emotions. Know that God is the mender of broken hearts and He will not fail you.

Facing Fear with Faith and Grace

The greatest moment in life is when we face fear and choose to move forward anyway. In my church, we say that fear is false evidence appearing real. I'm not sure who created that saying, but it is true. Fear makes it look like we are going to fail when in actuality, we have not even taken one step. Fear will discourage you before you even start the process but when you face your fear with faith, you give Jesus all of your worries and concerns.

The grace of God has already equipped you with everything you need to fulfill your purpose in this life. God has already considered your inadequacies and your weaknesses, and He still chose you to do something great in His kingdom. Fear would cause you to look at your weaknesses, but faith causes you to look to Jesus to fill those same inadequacies you see in yourself with His grace, power, and love.

When we depend on ourselves to do what God has called us to do, we will immediately be filled with fear. There is no humanly way possible that we can do anything that God has called us to do without God.

The Cure for Fear

Many of us are challenged with fear because we are unaware of just how much God loves us. The love of God cures fear because when you are confident in God's love for you, you are no longer afraid of what can happen to you. The truth is that God loves us so much, He sent His Son to die on the cross. So that we might have abundant life.

When I was driving through the Sierra Nevada Mountains, my confidence was not in the road or in my driving. My confidence was in God and His love for me. Because God loved me, I knew He would keep us safe. Because God loved me, I knew that He would ensure we were okay. I knew He would ensure that we got to the other side of the mountain safely.

God's greatest investment is you. Before you

were even created, God had a unique plan for your life because He loves you. There is nothing you could ever do to make Jesus stop loving you. Therefore, when you recognize that you are God's beloved, you walk in confidence that the same God who loves you is the same God who will ensure you make it into your destiny.

Chapter Summary

Fear paralyzes us from walking in our destiny. Whether the fear seems rational or irrational, the root of fear is aimed to destroy you. In the Word of God, it tells us to fear God, which means to reverence God, but we are not to be afraid of the God who loves us. The Bible clearly tells us that "God did not give us a spirit of fear, but of love and of a sound mind" (2 Timothy 1:7). If you have fear in your life, ask the Holy Spirit to examine your heart to find the root of your fear. The cure for all fear is God's perfect love. When you are perfected in Christ's love for you, there is nothing to be afraid of.

Study Scriptures

18 "There is no fear in love [dread does not exist]. But perfect (complete, full-grown) love drives out fear, because fear involves [the expectation of divine] punishment, so the one who is afraid [of God's judgment] is not perfected in love [has not grown into a sufficient understanding of God's love]."

1 John 4:18 (AMP)

27 "Peace I leave with you; My [perfect] peace I give to you; not as the world gives do I give to you. Do not let your heart be troubled, nor let it be afraid. [Let My perfect peace calm you in every circumstance and give you courage and strength for every challenge.]"

John 14:27 (AMP)

CHAPTER 8

Fissures of Failure

"God doesn't create failures."

Failure is not an option. In fact, you need to eliminate the word from your vocabulary today. Although we experience moments of failure, we are not failures in God's eyes. God's perspective of you is the only perspective that matters. When you aim to please God and please Him only, you learn to care a little less about how others perceive you.

For many of us, life has been difficult, throwing out unimaginable circumstances that have broken us into pieces changing our perspective of the world and ourselves. Circumstances can often influence decision-making. In the height of emotion, we can make decisions that propel or stagnate our future. Unfortunately, we usually pay a hefty price when our decisions have negative consequences. Everyone wants to be successful, but everyone at some point in life fails.

If I had a dollar for every time I thought about quitting, I would be rich. For every good idea I have, there are five thoughts to discourage that one idea. It is easier to give up and quit than it is to proceed. What often separates the successful from the unsuccessful, is the stamina to succeed or the determination to never give up.

Failure is a topic that is very close to my heart. At one point in my life, I believed that I was a failure. I felt that I had ruined everything good in my life. I told God He was wrong for believing in me because I felt so weak. The illusion of giving up can seem so desirable when you are at the end of yourself. It is easy to believe that the regret, doubt, pressure, pain, and frustration will leave if you just did not exist anymore. This battle is a difficult battle that takes place in the mind; it's the struggle of whether to continue or to stop.

No matter what is happening in your life, God has already equipped you with everything you need to be great in life. Sometimes, God needs us to come to the end of ourselves so that we only seek Him. Failure often takes place when we move ahead of God or out of His timing. When I look back over my life, every situation I have encountered that exhibited signs of failure happened because at some point, I made a move without God. If we give up when we are facing difficult situations, we forfeit God's divine intervention. It is often said that people quit right before a breakthrough. Meaning, we forfeit the opportunity of seeing God's manifestation right before it is about to happen.

Quitting is usually the first option the enemy presents to us whenever God instructs us. He knows that if he can get us to abandon the assignment God has given that he can keep us encaged in life—imprisoned in fear, regret, and condemnation. The whole concept of quitting is not from God. When God places a calling on your life, giving up before the process ends is not a factor. In fact, God has expectations that you will fulfill His purpose for your life.

In heaven, the enemy gave up. He had the opportunity to minister to God through music, but he wanted to be God. His position in music as an angel was an esteemed one filled with purpose and significance. Sadly, he quit his purpose in exchange for something that looked greater than his gift. In fact, how many times do we quit our gifts in an effort to mirror someone else's? When Satan chose to rebel against God, he cut himself off from the benefits of God.

We often consider the biting of the forbidden fruit as the greatest failure known. I would argue that the greatest failure was the moment Satan abandoned his purpose and assignment in heaven. When we abandon our purpose in anything, we are telling God that His will, His power, and His sacrifice of Jesus Christ is ultimately not enough. When we quit, we are showing God that our circumstance or failure is bigger than His ability to fix it, so we might as well quit.

When we believe that we are failures, it hinders our faith. Having a "failure mindset" breeds depression, discouragement, discontentment, confusion, frustration, and sorrow. You cannot think that you are a failure, yet, commit to fully trusting in God because in Christ we do not fail. We may make mistakes and learn from those mistakes to do better in the future, but we are not failures.

The truth is that there is nothing too big that our God is not equipped to handle. God was well aware of all of our future sins and mistakes when He sent Jesus to die on the cross for our past, present, and future sins. In fact, the love of God covers a multitude of sins, which includes all our dirt, shame, and secrets.

If we give up, we kill the opportunity of seeing the future result. If we quit at the bottom of the mountain, we forfeit the opportunity to see the view at the top of the mountain. If we kill the business idea in our heads before they have time to flourish, we kill the opportunity to see our ideas turn into franchises or million-dollar companies.

The Illusion of Failure

The enemy loves to create the illusion of failure—the illusion that God has failed you, forgotten you, or forsaken you. These are lies that the enemy uses to deepen your frustration with life to encourage you to embrace fear, hurt, loss, or frustration. In all truth, God has never left you or forgotten you. You are constantly on His mind.

God needs your faith in order to operate in your life. Our unbelief paralyzes God from moving in our lives. In the Bible, every miracle Jesus performed required faith. People were healed because of their faith and trust in God. Jesus does not pick and choose who He wants to help, but we do pick and choose who we will depend on in times of need. We can either look to God or look to the world. The choice is ours.

The Greatest Success

In your spiritual walk of faith, God has to be the only one you trust in. Satan comes to discredit and to dismantle God's purpose in your life. If he can get you to abort the process prematurely, he can get you to abort a dream or vision that may have changed the world if given the opportunity. The greatest failure that we can ever make in life is not realizing the power and authority we have in Jesus Christ.

When God leads your footsteps, you don't have to worry about mistakes, failures, or disappointments! Instead, you just walk in the freedom of God knowing that He is an unlimited resource. The Almighty is not restricted to the boundaries or limitations of this world. The only thing that can be restricted is our ability to dream and believe.

When we use our past experiences to define and label our future we embrace an automatic recipe for failure. Every situation is not always what it seems. What looks like a setback can often be a setup for something greater. Even in moments of failure, God could be building character or stamina within us for a greater blessing. Even when we do fail or make a mistake, God is there to pick up the pieces of our lives and rebuild us for the better. True success occurs when we trust God completely with everything we have to offer.

Rise Above (Poem)

I could sit all day and review my past, my failures, and
my mistakes
I could sit all day and dwell on the things I wish I
could change
I could sit all day and dwell on the negative, the issues,
the problems
I could sit all day and believe that my dreams are not
possible
Truth is, I've done all those things
Only to realize, that these things have further
constructed my passion for God
To love someone like me
To die for someone like me
To choose someone like me
To pursue someone like me
After all I've done
After all I've seen
I decided that if God could see the best for me
Then, I must rise above and see the best for myself.

-Alicia H. Watson-

Chapter Summary

God is not in the business of creating failures. When God looks at us, He sees us through the lens of Jesus Christ. There is no failure or bad choice that God cannot fix or give the grace to endure. When we mess up or fall short, it gives us another opportunity to totally trust God. God's love covers a multitude of sins and equips us with everything we need to be world changers. When you fail in life, take it to God and leave it at His feet. Shake yourself off and try again.

Study Scriptures

"I can do all things [which He has called me to do] through Him who strengthens and empowers me [to fulfill His purpose—I am self-sufficient in Christ's sufficiency; I am ready for anything and equal to anything through Him who infuses me with inner strength and confident peace."

Philippians 4:13 (AMP)

"Therefore let us [with privilege] approach the throne of grace [that is, the throne of God's gracious favor] with confidence and without fear, so that we may receive mercy [for our failures] and find [His amazing] grace to help in time of need [an appropriate blessing, coming just at the right moment]."

Hebrews 4:16 (AMP)

CHAPTER 9

Trusting Your Identity in God

"God made you in His image."

Your identity in Christ is crucial to your trust relationship with God. Knowing who you are and who you belong to shapes your identity, validity, and individuality in the world. If you want to know who you are, you have to go to the Creator to inquire about why you were designed. Too often, we look to the world to tell us who we are, what success is, and what we should desire. Seeking validation through the world will always end in rejection, but receiving confirmation through Christ will always end in acceptance.

We are Christlike. We are made in the image and likeness of God. Unlike God's other creations, we are made in His image. God designed us to mirror everything that He is. So, when He looks at us, He should be able to see His reflection in us. Our identity is a learned behavior. What you behold in life is what you will eventually become. The only way to find out who you are is to study the one who created you. When you study the life and heart of Jesus, you become like Jesus. Your life should mirror His love, His grace, His mercy, and His compassion. In our lives, it is easy to become focused on the wrong things, but God clearly wants us to focus on Him. As we focus on Him, He will give us wisdom and knowledge to handle everything else in our lives.

You Are Chosen, Created in His Image

You did not choose God, He chose you. God created you with the sole purpose of doing something unimaginable in your life. All He needs is your full cooperation in order to complete the very work in you that He has started. When I gave my life to Christ, I realized that God had His hand on me throughout every trial I have faced in my life. When I look back, I can see where God intentionally redirected my path so that I would eventually find comfort and wholeness in Him. I cannot take credit for where I am today without acknowledging the role that Jesus Christ has played in my life. And, I am sure that you cannot either.

God has adopted us into His family and has impregnated us with His DNA. God has selected us and given us the authority to rule the earth if we diligently seek Him. Being Godlike means that God has enabled us with the same power and authority that He gave His Son Jesus. Jesus healed the sick, raised the dead, and fed the hungry, which means we should walk in that same authority. Being means that

God handpicked you for this moment in time. God knew that He could trust you with the assignment that He has given you. We are a chosen people, a royal priesthood, and nothing can take that identity away from us.

Turning Pain into Purpose

The greatest decision I ever made in my spiritual walk was taking the focus off me. When I was the center, I was focused on how much hurt I suffered, how much pain I felt, and how much loss I had endured. Focusing on myself was debilitating because I was focused on why all of these bad things happened to me. Freedom came in my life when I took myself out of the center of my life and began to place Jesus in the center. Instead of focusing on what had happened to me, I began to focus on how God could use my experiences for His glory. This was the shift I needed to break out of all the fear, shame, and regret that held me back in life. I began to understand that God wanted to use my situation to minister to others and to set them free.

I do not know what your situation is or what you have experienced in life, but I do know that there is no problem, no past, no regret, or no shame that God cannot deliver you from. Your greatest weakness is often your greatest strength. Powerful ministry is always birthed from broken places. And, in your brokenness, God can put the pieces of your life back together fully integrated with His love and mercy. Your pain is what drives you into purpose. And, your purpose pushes you into your passion.

When we go through life without purpose, we are just living in mediocrity. God desires for us to have abundant life, which means a life full of joy, peace, love, mercy, compassion, and grace. The world will always have different labels and stereotypes to define you, but only God's opinion of you should matter. When we start to look to the world for acceptance and understanding, we open the door for the enemy to shape our perceptions. The world will never accept you completely because you were not designed to fit in. When God selected you, He marked you with His anointing. He called you to greater things than the world can ever offer.

Confidence in God

God requires us to be confident in His ability to do all things. When we eliminate the cracks, crevices, and dirt in our faith in God, we allow ourselves to completely trust Him to do exceedingly and abundantly above all we could ever ask or think. We should never compare ourselves with others because there is no comparison for God's unique design for you. When we are confident in who God has created us to be, we eliminate jealousy, envy, and hatred. When your foundation is built on God's Word, you destroy the enemy's plan to steal who you are. Many people spend their whole lives deceived into thinking that their identity is in something they were never designed to be. In fact, most people would rather spend their lives trying to become someone else, instead of asking God who they are.

The day that I stripped myself of everything I thought I was and should be, was the day that God told me who I was. In His presence, we can find answers to life's most challenging questions. Seeking God about who I was and who He created me to be affirmed my identity as a woman. The very things I saw as weaknesses in my life, God saw as strengths. God wanted to take all the things I was afraid of and make me victorious in those same areas. He took away all of my intellect and educational degrees, just to build Himself inside of me. Knowing that I was a daughter of God, a child of God with His power and anointing, gave me a completely new perspective of my life and purpose. God does not need your qualifications or accomplishments, but He does need a willing heart. Trusting God with a willing heart means that you are open to whatever journey God has for you. God has planted something phenomenal in you and He is waiting for you to completely trust in Him and His process.

Chapter Summary

When we eliminate Satan's influence in our lives, we open the door to spiritual awakening and breakthrough. God desires to mirror Himself in you as you show others His grace, mercy, love, compassion, and power. As believers, we have to learn to only see Jesus in our lives. God will take care of the rest. However, when we focus on Jesus, we focus on His ability to do everything we need instead of our own ability. Trusting solely in God is keeping your focus on the problem-solver, not the problem itself. Whatever you focus on will be greater in your eyes and whatever you do not focus on will not bring attention to itself. God needs open access to your heart in order for His will and plan to be fully implemented in your life. Knowing our identity in God leads us into our purpose, where passion is ignited. Spending quality time in God's Word and presence will always give us the answers and confidence we need to know that God is more than able to perfect everything that concerns us.

Study Scriptures

"So God created man in His own image, in the image and likeness of God He created him; male and female He created them."

Genesis 1:27 (AMP)

"But you are a chosen race, a royal priesthood, a consecrated nation, a [special] people for God's own possession, so that you may proclaim the excellencies [the wonderful deeds and virtues and perfections] of Him who called you out of darkness into His marvelous light."

1 Peter 2:9 (AMP)

CHAPTER 10

Belief Breakthrough

"When we believe in God confidently, we yield Godlike results."

Throughout my life, I have experienced many situations that tested my belief and trust in God. I have shared with you many of those experiences, but I have one more story to tell. A few years ago, I had a severe battle with depression. No one knew except my close friends. I was functional, meaning I still went to church and work, I served on the praise team, and on the outside, I looked happy. While on the inside, I was hurting and would often cry myself to sleep. I would tell friends and family members that my eyes were swollen from allergies, but they were really swollen from what felt like an ocean of tears. I was so unhappy with life, and I wanted to give up. In fact, I was ready to die and end what seemed like a horrid life. During this period of about 6 months, I could not seem to find joy in anything. Every good moment was scarred with the thoughts of what I was going through.

My depression had not only affected my mind but my health as well. I was extremely tired and fatigued and nothing really seemed to help. I could only focus on the negative things that were happening around me and the regret for where I felt I should have been in life. I magnified my problems feeling that they were impossible to solve. I isolated myself thinking that I had to fix whatever was broken inside of me. Out of everything I've been through, that season of my life was the hardest. I was living without purpose and wandering in my decisions hoping I would find the right road to success. I dreamed of escaping the pain and failure I felt because all of my great decisions landed me in a place of chaos and confusion. I wanted to quit on God and on life.

Now, you may ask, how does a Christian get to such a low place? Well, in my case, every situation I was facing seemed impossible. I began focusing on my debt, my deteriorating health, and all the problems that were around me. I was consumed by all of my problems and lack of solutions. When I went to church, I would find myself downing or not receiving the message. I would say things like "Oh, God's favor doesn't apply to me anymore! I've messed up too badly!" Life was just life. Before I knew it, I was barely myself and I had lost my identity in God. Fortunately, it was in my depression that God birthed the title of this book. My life was failing because I had stopped trusting in God's ability over my own ability. I was looking at how I was going to fix my problems instead of putting everything I was lacking in His hands and trusting Him with it. I was carrying the weight of life without casting my cares on Jesus. I was drowning in sorrow because I chose to hold on to situations and problems that I could not fix. This situation uncovered all the cracks, crevices, and dirt that were embedded in my faith. When I look back, I realize, that God was exposing every lie, so that I could deal with it and be free.

Over a few months, God started waking me up in the middle of the night to address areas where I lacked trust in Him. In those moments, with the gentleness of the Holy Spirit, God showed me the root issues in my belief system. He unrooted lies in my mind like "I am a failure" and "I've ruined my life. "God began taking me to His Word to re-establish my identity in Him. Through this process, I felt like God was ripping me apart only to put me back together—better than before. I had to face the pain of my childhood, the loss of my parents, the dysfunction of my teenage years, and the religious thinking I had developed about God. I had to be completely vulnerable before God and deal with the secret issues of my heart.

Although the process was painful, it was temporary. As God dealt with me, I noticed my joy and my laughter returning. I was becoming free day by day, and it was beautiful. I learned that before I evolved into the woman God wanted me to be, I had to face the woman and the little girl I used to be. God needed me to confront every issue that was preventing me from relying on Him in my life. It was so freeing to learn that God cared nothing about my mistakes. He wasn't concerned about all of my sin and shame, and He wasn't concerned with all of my bad choices. He did not care about the impossibilities that I faced because He was bigger than all of those things.

Believe Only

More than anything, God needs your trust in Him. You do not have to have the answers for your life because God has the answers for your life. In Him lies everything that you need—already prepared for your arrival. Focusing on the past or what is currently happening in your life, limits God from moving supernaturally in your situation. At some point as believers, we actually have to choose to believe what God says. It's one thing to hear His promises, but it's another thing to confidently believe that His promises are obtainable through our faith and belief. If you feel like you are losing in life, it's not God who has failed you, it's your belief. Success in God's kingdom requires the absolute abandonment of the world's system.

When we fail in life, it is often because we are trying to work God's system and the world's system at the same time. The systems of the world and of heaven are completely different. When we believe God only, we believe in His principles and His methods of promotion. God promotes us when our hearts are positioned in a humble place for us to receive what He has for us. The world promotes us when we work harder, sometimes, to our own detriment. There are many people in the world who are so consumed with work that they forget to enjoy their life or spend time with those they love. God desires for us to have abundant life, which includes our fulfillment as individuals. When we stand on God's Word, we position ourselves for miraculous results.

God has given us the power and the authority to speak and to create the world we desire to see. No matter how many issues we face in life, God has given us the authority to overcome anything and everything that comes our way. When we speak the Word of God (out loud) with power and assurance, we take our rightful place as heirs of Jesus Christ. Speaking the Word of God with authority gives us the confidence that whatever we ask for in Jesus' name will be manifested in our lives.

After realizing the cracks and crevices in my own faith, nothing changed until I took authority over my own life. I began to realize that the power of my destiny lies in my belief and in what I say. If I speak and believe that all is well, then all will be well. But, if I speak negatively, my perspective will become pessimistic, only allowing me to focus on the negative. I know that my words have to align with what I believe. God desires for me to be in one accord with His Word, my faith in Him, and His promises toward me. The three of these things manifested together breed unlimited power and strength. God has given us all the power to rule in this life, but we must align ourselves with His kingdom principles. We have what we say, we speak what we believe, and we manifest the supernatural results.

Keep Jesus at the Center

Focus: The ability to streamline all thoughts and energy into one direction. - AHW

In life, we have to examine our focus. We have to ask ourselves: Where am I looking? What am I doing? What am I putting all of my energy into? Am I living in my purpose? Where is the stress in my life coming from? Am I spending quality time with God and His Word? Am I walking on the path that God has designed for me or am I trying to walk on someone else's pathway? Am I tired or frustrated? What are the areas of my life I can change and what are the areas I need God to change?

In our pursuit of happiness in life, we can become distracted by all the things that pull on our mental, emotional, and physical energy. Although it is good to analyze life in certain moments, sometimes God requires us to just stop and listen to Him. In I Peter 5:7, the Word tells us to cast all of our cares upon God—living carefree because He cares for us. Can you imagine a carefree life?

In fact, can you imagine living a life where all of your focus and energy is mainstreamed into your relationship with Jesus? When we give Jesus everything, we eliminate the failure in our lives. Jesus is concerned with your everyday affairs and has readily available wisdom for every situation you encounter. Well, when we lose focus of Him, we invite cracks into our beliefs and faith.

When we allow ourselves to rest in Jesus, we wholeheartedly believe that God has already provided everything we need for our entire lives. We rest in the knowledge that His love and grace are sufficient for any situation that we may encounter and that in His presence all weights and burdens are lifted. When you place Jesus first, everything in your life will begin to fall into its correct place. Inviting God to participate in your day, allows His will to flourish in your life for others to see. Even in your imperfections, God is able to work on your weaknesses transforming them into strengths. Every time I have taken control of my own life, I have fallen flat on my face broken from my mistakes. But, when Jesus is my focus, I soar through life realizing that all of my help, happiness, joy, peace, love, and rest come directly from my heavenly Father.

Chapter Summary

When we keep Jesus at the center of our lives, we eliminate all distractions from the enemy. Staying focused on the problem-solver lessens the magnitude of the problem we are facing. Speaking God's Word over our situations is the gateway to breakthrough and deliverance. Believing solely in what God has said and His promises give us the tools we need to focus on our future and not our past or present. When we eliminate the lies that prevent us from trusting God, we create a foundation of trust and expectation between ourselves and our relationship with Christ. When we choose to believe in God and His Word only, we expose and eliminate every lie that prevents us from trusting in God.

Study Scriptures

"I assure you and most solemnly say to you, whoever says to this mountain, 'Be lifted up and thrown into the sea!' and does not doubt in his heart [in God's unlimited power], but believes that what he says is going to take place, it will be done for him [in accordance with God's will]."

Mark 11:23 (AMP)

"Yet we have the same spirit of faith as he had, who wrote in Scripture, "I believed, therefore I spoke." We also believe, therefore we also speak."

2 Corinthians 4:13 (AMP)

ABOUT THE AUTHOR

Born in 1984, Alicia had no idea of the life that would be before her. The only daughter of the late John E. Watson and Esther Bell-Watson, Alicia was destined for greatness from the beginning. Being blessed by the late Pope John Paul in Rome, Italy, was not only a blessing but a reminder of God's hand on her life. After losing her father at the age of 10, and burying her mother on her 15th birthday, Alicia made a commitment to herself and to God to inspire the world. Although she has faced great tragedies throughout her life, Alicia is determined to re-present the loving heart of God to the world.

Currently, she has the amazing opportunity to serve as a member of the praise team at World Changers Church International under the dynamic leadership of Dr. Creflo Dollar and Pastor Taffi Dollar. Recently, she released her debut single "New Mercy" on iTunes, Amazon, and Google Play (available for download today). Alicia loves to sing and write to encourage and inspire people about he the love and mercy of God. Using her story as a platform, Alicia was recently a guest on the Your World With Creflo Dollar Television Show, where she shared in-depth details about growing up with deadly family secrets.

As Alicia further develops into purpose and passion, she is excited about the future God has planned for her. She currently blogs and writes on her website, www.aliciahulene.org. Alicia is committed to traveling the world to speak to people about God's love and overcoming impossibilities in life.